Reconsidering
Read-Aloud

Reconsidering Read-Aloud

MARY LEE HAHN

Stenhouse Publishers
Portland, Maine

Stenhouse Publishers
www.stenhouse.com

Library of Congress Cataloging-in-Publication Data
Hahn, Mary Lee, 1960–
    Reconsidering read-aloud / Mary Lee Hahn.
    p. cm.
Includes bibliographical references.
    ISBN 1-57110-351-1 (alk. paper)
    1. Children—Books and reading—United States. 2. Oral reading. 3. Reading (Middle school)—United States. 4. Children's literature—Study and teaching (Middle school)—United States. I. Title.
Z1037.A1 H25 2002
028.5'5—dc21   2002075795

Cover and interior photographs for Chapters 1–2, 4–7 by Aloysius J. Wald

Manufactured in the United States of America on acid-free paper
08 07 06 05 04 03 02 9 8 7 6 5 4 3 2 1

*Dedicated to the people
who read to me first:
my mom, my dad,
and my big brother.*

Contents

Acknowledgments

Wisdom tells me I am nothing;
love tells me I am everything.
Between the two, my life flows.
—An Indian master

When Franki Sibberson and Karen Szymusiak asked me to do my presentation on read-aloud for the class they were teaching, I agreed, if for no other reason than to have them in my audience. Over the last ten or fifteen years, we have worked together on committees, planned conferences together, and even launched a book club, but I had never had the opportunity to teach with them. I value their professional opinions. In fact, as I walked up the steps of the school where I would be presenting, I said to myself, "If Franki says, 'You should write a book,' I'll do it." Obviously, she said it. Thanks for getting me started, Franki.

Franki wasn't the only one who believed in me early on. Thank you to my editor, Bill Varner, and the folks at Stenhouse who saw something in those early drafts that told them I was worth the risk.

There couldn't have been a book at all if it hadn't been for my students. All of you, from the first class at W. A. Blair Elementary in Dallas, Texas, to the classes at Deer Run Elementary and Daniel Wright Elementary in Dublin, Ohio, have helped me become the teacher I am today. Every day is new and alive and important when you walk through the classroom door all smart and funny, ornery and unpredictable, compassionate and patient, and ready like sponges to learn. A special thanks to your parents for letting me be a part of your families for a little while.

I'm glad I let Charlotte Huck talk me into interviewing with the Dublin City Schools when I finished my master's degree, and I'm glad they hired me. This is a district filled with forward-thinking administrators and teachers. My classroom has developed into the child-centered, literature-based place it is now in large part because of the rich environment in which I have taught and learned for the last sixteen years. A special thanks to four of the amazing teachers I've been blessed to work with over the years: Karen Terlecky, Joyce Zawaly, Julia Barthelmes, and Carol Wiltse, whose read-aloud stories from their third-, fourth-, fifth-, and sixth-grade classrooms made this book so much richer. Thanks also to the sixty-seven Dublin elementary and middle school teachers who responded enthusiastically to my call for favorite read-alouds.

Another gift I received early in my career was an invitation from Janet Hickman to join the team of teachers who produced *The W.E.B*, a former Ohio State University publication that contained reviews of children's books and offered in each issue a web of ideas for using children's literature in the classroom. For ten years I was informally apprenticed to a group of very smart and extremely talented master teachers—the best of the best. It was from them that I really learned how to think about, talk about, write about, and teach with children's literature. Thank you all.

I allowed myself to let magazines and professional journals pile up while I wrote this book, but I promised myself that I would keep up with my book club reading no matter what. Thank you to Lisa, Sharon, Lynn, Josie, Sue, and Mary Kate for that monthly island of sanity. Thanks also to the kids and parents in this year's class book club, and to each of my parent/child book clubs throughout the years, especially the one that lasted from *The Talking Earth* in fourth grade to *The Count of Monte Cristo* in ninth grade. I am also thankful for the informal book clubs in my life— the impromptu ones at the lunch table in the teachers' lounge, or at the copier, or in the hallway before the students come. A thank-you to all of the readers in my life.

Thank you to A. J. Wald for photographing my class during read-aloud. I appreciate the time you took from your own writing to come and serve as another pair of eyes. But that's just the tip of the iceberg. Thanks also for being the first reader of, or listener to, every draft of every chapter of this book. It is a better book because of you. Thank you for all of our conversations about the art of writing and the mystery of the process. You understood, often better than I did, when I needed to be left alone to work and when I needed to stop for a dog walk and coffee at Stauf's. I am a better writer because of you. Most of all, thank you for your unfailing belief in me, for being patient with all my quirks and moods, and for being there through fourteen years of thick and thin. Together we looked death in the face, and then went fly-fishing. I am a better person because of you.

Learning
Without Trying

It is read-aloud time. The classroom is absolutely silent except for my voice and the muffled sounds of children playing on the playground that come in along with the puffs of fresh air through the open window. Some students sit with their chins propped up in a cupped hand; others lay their heads on their desks. Every student is relaxed yet alert. There is tension in the air, a simultaneous yearning for closure and for continuation. Some watch me. Others stare into space. Because they are each intently visualizing the story in their own way, the eyes of all the students seem slightly out of focus.

My eyes are the eyes of all twenty-six students as I read the book. My voice paints the story on the canvas of twenty-six imaginations. The story can pause for a question, a comment, or a short discussion to clarify or extend meaning without the spell being broken. Even when the book is closed at the end of a chapter or the end of the book, and the room erupts into cries for more or sighs of satisfaction, the magic of read-aloud is not gone. An individual connection has been forged between me and each student via the book. Just like a parent at the edge of the bed or with the child in my lap, my voice has personally delivered the story directly to each pair of ears and each imagination. The book also creates a collective connection, bonding me and all the students together as one through the common experience of having met the same characters, gone on the same journeys, and suffered the same losses and triumphs.

Read-aloud may look like an ordinary event in a typical classroom, but it feels extraordinary when the teacher who is reading is aware of the power of the book and the importance of her role in not only reading to her students, but leading them through the book—using read-aloud as a teaching time. Not only the teacher can feel the difference, but also the students. At the end of one school year when I asked my students to reflect on our read-aloud time, Mathias captured the essence of read-aloud in our classroom when he wrote, "It is a time when we can learn without trying."

From the student's perspective, read-aloud in our classroom is an enjoyable learning time. It is learning "without trying" because it is rarely tied to paper-and-pencil tasks, and the learning is never formally tested. The basic expectation for participation is quite low—everyone should listen—so with every book, nearly every student exceeds the expectations by becoming deeply involved in the story and sometimes passionately active in the discussions. Students love read-aloud because it seems easy. For one thing, they do not have to work by themselves to construct meaning: read-aloud is a whole-class collaboration. Also, learning comes naturally during read-aloud because it comes by listening, questioning, speaking, and visualizing—the first ways a child acquires language and learns about stories. Ideally, many of the students have had years of experience listening to and talking about stories that have been read aloud by their parents, older brothers and sisters, baby-sitters, and primary-grade teachers. By the time they get to the middle grades, read-aloud should be a familiar and cherished time in the school day for students.

As the teacher, read-aloud is enjoyable for me as well. Read-aloud is when I can share my love of books and reading with the whole class. During read-aloud I can practice my otherwise underutilized acting abilities by reading with expression and drama. The role of teacher/authority figure often sets me apart from my students, but read-aloud provides me the opportunity to be an equal part of our classroom community. It is a time when we all laugh and cry and discuss together. Read-aloud is also an enjoyable teaching time for me. In fact, I do some of my best teaching during read-aloud. During read-aloud I am free to practice the art of teaching; during read-aloud, I am not limited by manuals, ditto sheets, or purchased curriculums. I teach from the very core of my being, drawing upon my every experience, as well as upon my wide range of reading and study. I am guided by, but not limited by, national and state standards, proficiency outcomes, and my local graded courses of study. During read-aloud, I am rewarded with richly teachable moments when I choose just the right books. Likewise, my opportunities for good teaching during read-aloud increase proportionally to how well I know my students and how willing I am to follow where they lead my teaching.

Read-aloud lends itself well to artful teaching. The few ingredients—a reader, a book, and listeners—belie simplicity. For an artist, a few simple ingredients represent infinite potential. The basic ingredients of read-aloud represent infinite teaching and learning opportunities, especially in a classroom where literacy is valued, promoted, taught, expected, and modeled every day, all day long. In the literacy-rich classroom of an artful teacher, read-aloud is not a discrete activity. It is deeply embedded in teaching and learning throughout the day, the unit, or the year. Each book is thoughtfully chosen to support the skills the students are acquiring in their own reading, their own writing, or their own thinking and learning. Read-aloud books are chosen to add depth or perspective to what is being learned in social studies, science, health, or mathematics. To help students mature, books are chosen for read-aloud that will provide windows into other lives, as well as mirrors that reflect the familiar, and that explore the myriad of ways humans respond to life's challenges. To describe read-aloud in a literacy-rich classroom is to describe one strand in a tapestry of teaching, in which read-aloud is woven into the classroom community, the reading and writing workshops, and the teaching that is part of every classroom event.

Any art takes time and practice to develop. I have been studying the art of teaching for nearly twenty years. I have known since the very beginning of my career that read-aloud holds a special and important place in the classroom routine. I took my first lessons from Charlotte Huck:

> Unfortunately, the practice of a daily story hour is not as common in the middle grades as in the primary grades. Yet, we know that it is just as essential. Reading comprehension is improved as students listen to and discuss events, characters and motivation. They learn to predict what will happen. They increase their vocabulary. This is the time that the teacher can introduce children to various genres of books like historical fiction, fantasy, biography, and poetry, which the children might not be reading.
>
> Primarily, however, the read-aloud time will cause children to want to read. Once a child has heard a good book read aloud, he or she can hardly wait to savor it again. Reading aloud thus generates further interest in books. Good oral reading should develop a taste for fine literature. (Huck, Hepler, and Hickman 1987, p. 644)

About midway through my career, read-aloud began to emerge from the landscape of my teaching as more than just a routine daily event. I distinctly remember the time my principal popped into my room for an unannounced observation just as I was beginning read-aloud. I briefly considered rearranging the schedule so that she could "see me teaching," but as soon as I had that thought, I knew that I *was* teaching, and that I could trust the book to provide us with questions, predictions, and conversations that would show my principal all the teaching and learning that took place during my read-aloud.

In the last several years, I have begun to consider read-aloud an essential and central component in the teaching of reading in my classroom. When I began to focus my constant and critical attention on read-aloud, I was amazed to discover teaching I hadn't realized I was doing and learning that had likewise escaped my notice. The epiphany came during an in-service workshop on the outcomes for the fourth- and sixth-grade Ohio Proficiency Tests. Based on those outcomes, I started jotting down a list of all the skills and strategies I could think of that I had taught in any way, shape, or form during read-aloud. I thought back on my book choices, our discussions, and the quick, spontaneous interjections I made to highlight or model reading skills and strategies. The longer my list grew, the clearer the pattern became: I had touched upon nearly every one of our state's proficiency outcomes in reading for fourth and sixth grades. When I cross-checked my list with the reading strategies in Stephanie Harvey and Anne Goudvis's *Strategies That Work* (2000), I found that I had modeled nearly every one of those strategies as well. My original list included the following:

Book choice
Book clues/first predictions
Remember where you left off—monitoring
Retelling
Summarizing
Connections
Response
Reading with expression
Vocabulary in context
Rereading for sense—monitoring
Nonfiction structures and strategies
Deciding what to read next

Inferring/predicting based on the text

Author's purpose

How the contents and/or structure of the text support the author's
purpose

At almost the same time that I discovered this gold mine of teaching
that I was doing during read-aloud, I was given the language to name the
instructional strategies I was using. I had the opportunity to help develop
a Framework for Literacy for our school district. The intent of the
framework is to give our teachers a common language for our shared
instructional philosophy. Elements of the framework, such as reading and
writing workshop, were familiar to me. But one strand, the Apprenticeship
Model, has changed the way I teach and the way I look at my read-aloud.

The Apprenticeship Model, which our Framework Committee created, was inspired by the real-life out-of-school teaching and learning situations described in *Situated Learning: Legitimate Peripheral Participation*
(Lave and Wenger 1991). In particular, the account of the apprenticeship
of tailors in Liberia helped us organize four important elements we had
identified for our teaching of literacy. Our Apprenticeship Model links
four common instructional strategies into a chain of teaching in which
the expert gradually releases control and support until the apprentice can
perform the skill independently:

1. modeling, when the teacher does all the work,
2. shared learning, when the students have some input with lots of
   teacher support,
3. guided learning, when the students, often working in groups or
   pairs, have most of the input with some teacher support, and
4. independent application of the skill, when the students are able to
   complete the task without teacher support.

When I held up the Apprenticeship Model to read-aloud, it was as if
the optometrist had clicked into place the lens that makes it all clear. I
could see what a powerful place read-aloud has in all the reading instruction I do throughout the day. It functions first and foremost as a model
for students. Now I am aware that during every moment of every read-
aloud I am teaching students something about reading, from basic book
handling all the way to being so emotionally moved by a story that I

laugh or cry out loud. Now I pay close attention to every moment of the read-aloud and consider what I am modeling about reading.

Read-aloud is also a powerful shared learning time. The discussions I lead before, during, or after reading aloud can give students the opportunity to test new ways of thinking with plenty of support from me.

When I invite students to turn to a neighbor or meet in small groups to discuss the read-aloud book as I circulate and listen in or add my two cents, I am giving them guided experience in thinking and talking about books and reading—guided by their peers as much as, or more than, guided by me.

During independent reading time in reading workshop, students have the opportunity to try using what they've learned during read-aloud. When we reach the independent phase of lessons in other subjects, the students are often evaluated or graded on how well they can perform a skill. Independently using what is learned during read-aloud in one's own reading is much less threatening because the assessment of success in reading is cumulative, rather than terminal. When adding two plus three in math, it is mandatory that you come up with five. When analyzing characters in reading, you become more and more critical and insightful, but there is never one single correct answer that works every time.

So read-aloud is an enjoyable time for both students and teachers. It is a time rich for teaching and ripe for learning. A broad continuum of reading activities can be considered a read-aloud. At one end of the continuum is pure entertainment—students simply listening to a story read aloud by the teacher. At the other end of the continuum is shared reading—a read-aloud in which each student follows along in a copy of the text. For the purpose of this book, I will focus on the middle of the continuum of read-aloud purposes: when read-aloud is more than just a quiet time when students are entertained by listening to a story, but less than a shared reading experience in which they follow along in their own copy of the text. In the middle of the continuum is a read-aloud dually devoted to enjoyment and to reading instruction.

The first three chapters will explore the basic elements of an effective read-aloud: the teacher, the books, and the classroom community. The chapters on general strategies, fiction strategies, and nonfiction strategies will provide examples that demonstrate how teaching is spontaneously and unobtrusively woven into read-aloud, and the importance of inquiry—letting the teaching follow where the students lead. Finally, the assessment of learning in read-aloud will be addressed.

1

The Roles
of the Teacher

When you read aloud to your class, you are modeling the skills and strategies of a proficient reader. At the most basic level, there's not much more to read-aloud than that. However, this incidental or accidental modeling can be transformed into powerful teaching when it is done intentionally and authentically. The only way to authentically model those skills and strategies is to use them yourself: to teach reading well, you must know it from the inside out. Therefore, the most important role of the reading teacher is that of role model.

As the role model reader, you must be a reader yourself—a metacognitive reader who talks about and owns books—and you must wear the role of reader on your sleeve so that there is no question in your students' minds who you are and what you stand for when it comes to books.

Be a Reader

It is critical for a teacher of reading to be a reader. A study by Postlethwaite and Ross (1992) found that

> teacher readership of literature (novels, poems, plays, and children's books), informational texts (books on history, art, and science), and professional materials (articles and books on teaching and reading) were significant factors that were associated with student reading achievement. That is, teachers who reported reading for their own purposes—for pleasure, for information, for professional development—had students who tended to be more advanced in literacy learning than students coming from classrooms in which their teachers were less likely to read for their own purposes. (in Rasinski 2001, p. 84)

Read-aloud in the classroom of a teacher who is a reader is a rich experience. You can't share the adult books and authors that you love with your students, but the value you personally place on books and reading is made evident in hundreds of subtle ways during read-aloud and the talk that surrounds and is a part of read-aloud. Maybe you mention trips to bookstores and libraries. Or you share that you are a little tired because you stayed up late finishing a book. Perhaps your love of reading and books is evident in the way you handle books so carefully. Your enthusiasm for books is apparent when you excitedly share the newest books by your favorite authors. You might set reading goals and show your students the annotated list of all the books you read each year.

Whether or not you are a reader of adult books, you should, as a teacher of reading, be a voracious reader of children's books. Whatever your students are reading, you should be reading. For one class, that meant that my reading spanned from the Little Bill series to Brian Jacques's *Redwall*, and encompassed everything in between. Many years

ago, a colleague with an amazingly wide knowledge of children's literature and children's authors impressed me with her offhand remark that
she usually read at least one children's novel a week. Because I so admired
her knowledge of children's literature, I resolved in 1987 to try to read
fifty-two children's books that year. Over the last fifteen years, that resolution has evolved to fifty-two children's books and twenty adult books. It
is the only New Year's resolution that I consistently keep, and one of the
best and most enjoyable professional development activities in which I
have ever participated. The payoff has been huge—knowing most of the
books and authors my students are reading independently, and discovering great new read-alouds. Julia Barthelmes teaches fifth grade next door
to me. Several years ago, she set the goal of reading every Newbery book,
a goal I so admire that I may borrow it the way I did the "children's novel
a week" goal. Her knowledge of the best books in children's literature
informs both her teaching of reading—her Newbery unit is extraordinary
in depth because she can practically handpick books for children—and
her choices for read-aloud.

At the end of each school year, I have a series of written and spoken
conversations with my students to try to discover if what I thought I was
teaching during read-aloud was what they actually learned. Along with
the hoped-for responses about reading skills and strategies, I find facets
of my love of reading reflected in their comments.

Stories have always come to life in my head, in pictures and sounds
and even smells. (I remember once as a child reading a book about pio-
neers. It was right before dinner, and my mouth watered at the description of fresh meat cooking over the open fire. I ran to the kitchen and
begged Mom to cook us "plain meat" for dinner.) Because I am a reader
for whom stories come to life, my students in their responses said they
loved the way I brought stories to life for them, reading with expression,
and, as one child said, "how you do the voices and exclamation points."
Because I am a reader, I know the power of the cliffhanger, and I passed
that on to Lizzy, who loved it when "we get to a really good part and then
you stop right in the middle." Being a reader myself also helped me to
"choose books we would *never* pick," something that impressed Ashleigh.
Similarly, Kevin appreciated that I encouraged the students to "stretch
out to different authors."

I model the role of reader outside of read-aloud as well. I belong to
two book clubs. I am host of a book club for my students and their parents.

In the course of our conversations, I invariably tell my students about the books I am reading with my other book club, my adult book club, and they hear me sharing adult book titles and authors with their parents in the informal times before and after book club. When we talk about our reading habits early in the year, I bring in the piles of books and magazines and professional journals that I keep at my bedside. When we read the newspaper, I share my "Craig Wilson File"—several years' worth of Wilson's Wednesday column clipped from *USA Today*—and I encourage them to find a favorite columnist or section or even comic in the paper to look forward to, like meeting an old friend. Books and reading are a huge part of my world, and I intentionally model for my students how they can make reading and books a part of their lives.

Be a Metacognitive Reader

I am a reader, and I bring my love of books and story to read-aloud. More important, I am a metacognitive reader. I think about my own thinking while I read and while I read aloud. As Ellin Keene puts it, "I have moved from a passive to an active stance. I am acutely aware of my own reading process, the questions and challenges I have for the authors I read, the awareness I have of moments of confusion and disorientation in the text, and the tools I use to confront that confusion" (Keene and Zimmerman 1997, p. 5). When I was a child learning to read, no one ever formally introduced me to this voice in my head that would say, "Huh?" when I read something confusing, or "You can't *do* that!" to the author when once again the dog in the story died. Somehow I made it all the way through college without a close relationship with the voice in my head when I read. It was in graduate school, when I studied the teaching of reading in more depth, and in the years of teaching beyond graduate school, when I was working to refine my teaching of reading, that I gradually discovered the power of conversing with that voice in my head—the power of metacognition.

Read-aloud provides the perfect opportunity for modeling a metacognitive approach to reading. My students can see me using the reading comprehension strategies identified by research as those that proficient readers use as they read: activating prior knowledge, determining the most important ideas in a text, asking questions, visualizing, inferring, synthesizing, and using fix-up strategies when comprehension breaks down (Keene and Zimmerman 1997, pp. 22–23). Without allowing my comments to interfere with the flow of the story, I might interject such quick thoughts as

> "I've heard about that before, have you?" (activating prior knowledge)
> "Is that a topic sentence, or what?" (determining the most important ideas in a text)
> "What just happened?" (asking questions)
> "Can't you picture that!? What do you see?" (visualization)
> "What do you make of those clues the author just gave us?" (inferring)
> "Hey, isn't this just like that story we read in the newspaper yesterday?" (synthesizing) and
> "Wait a minute. I didn't read that right. Let me read it over again." (using fix-up strategies when comprehension breaks down)

Comprehension is a complex balance of skills and strategies that are used simultaneously in ever-changing combinations and amounts.

> There is no one way to teach for comprehension. Note that we tend to insert the preposition *for* to remind us that comprehension takes place in the brain of the reader. We can bring an effective technique (for example, noticing an author's ability to evoke images) to students' attention, but we cannot give it to them directly. They must construct a network of techniques for themselves. (Fountas and Pinnell 2001, p. 323)

Read-aloud is the perfect time to provide students with a window into the comprehension of a proficient reader so that they can begin to "construct a network of techniques for themselves."

Talk About Books and Reading

Readers talk to other readers about books. It's just what we do. Sometimes we talk superficially: "What are you reading now? How do you like it?" Sometimes we watch other people talk about books on Oprah or CNN's *Booknotes*. We read reviews to hear someone else's thoughts about books. We join virtual book clubs, such as the one at BookCrossing.com, and live book clubs and talk for hours around restaurant tables and coffee house tables and bookstore tables and kitchen tables. Talking about books is part of reading.

Every time we talk about books with another reader, both of us come away better readers (not to mention armed with another title to add to our list of books to read). Consider the higher-level thinking and reading skills required to talk to your friend about the book you just finished: talk about books often involves giving concise plot summaries, requires forming and expressing opinions, and necessitates making connections between the text, yourself, the other reader, other books, and the world. When the whole class is involved in discussions of the read-aloud book, each of the students is becoming a better reader. Talking about the read-aloud also changes the way students listen. When asked, "What happens inside your brain during read-aloud?" Ashleigh answered, "I think about connections and things to say." She applies this in her independent reading by "stopping and talking about it or thinking about what happens."

Teachers can promote better talk during read-aloud discussions by asking better questions. Literal questions (who, where, when) shut down a discussion with a single right answer. "Literary questions raise the level of discussion and often begin with *why, what do you think, how, discuss, describe.* A literary question prompts readers to consider multiple possibilities, examine the text more carefully, raise additional questions, and listen to other points of view" (Routman 2000, p. 183). The very best questions are the ones the teacher does not have the answer for. These are authentic questions that the teacher and class can explore together as equals.

Own Books

Readers own books, treasure books, value books. Books help us understand the world around us, both through information and through stories. The kinds of books we choose for our classrooms and to share with our students during read-aloud can change their lives—and ours, too.

> In books I have traveled, not only to other worlds, but into my own. I learned who I was and who I wanted to be, what I might aspire to, and what I might dare to dream about my world and myself. More powerfully and persuasively than from the "shalt nots" of the Ten Commandments, I learned the difference

between good and evil, right and wrong. One of my favorite childhood books, *A Wrinkle in Time*, described that evil, that wrong, existing in a different dimension from our own. But I felt that I, too, existed much of the time in a different dimension from everyone else I knew. There was waking, and there was sleeping. And then there were books, a kind of parallel universe in which anything might happen and frequently did, a universe in which I might be a newcomer but was never really a stranger. My real, true world. My perfect island. (Quindlen 1998, p. ii)

If someone walked into your house, could they tell by looking that you are an avid reader—that you also are a frequent visitor to the "parallel universe" in books? Does your décor revolve around bookcases of all sizes? Are there piles of newspapers and magazines to be seen? Is there reading material in every room of the house? How tall are the stacks beside your bed? (Multiply all those images when two or more readers are living in the same house.) Avid readers own lots of books. Some are books for the future—bought on a sort of "reading insurance plan"— books purchased to be taken home and placed on a special shelf with other books that are to be read "someday." Some are books from the past—the most life-changing books kept from college and high school and middle school. The books a reader owns are visible mile markers of a lifetime journey of reading, thinking, and learning.

Avid readers "collect" bookstores like avid coffee drinkers "collect" coffeehouses in every city they visit. A reader can pick which bookstore to visit based on the book they need, the mood they're in, or how long they want to browse. Readers recommend bookstores like wine drinkers recommend vintages. Some bookstores, like the Tattered Cover in Denver, are worthy of a yearly pilgrimage.

Teachers who are avid readers have classrooms overflowing with books. Anyone who walks into their classroom can tell by looking that they love books and value reading. Teachers who are readers are incredibly ingenious in the ways they fill their classrooms with books. They hit garage sales, scour library sales, ask for donations, use up book-order bonus points, and write grants to fill their classrooms with books.

Not every child we teach comes from a house filled with books, but a classroom—their home away from home—that is filled with books can be the place where they first practice living as a reader.

Put Read-Aloud at the Heart of Reading Instruction

As a role model reader, you make evident the personal value you place on reading. You are a metacognitive reader who talks about and owns books. Your next role is more professional in nature, yet the value you place on reading is strongly evident: you must put read-aloud at the heart of your reading instruction.

> How important is reading aloud? Critically important. "Don't you ever want kids to just lie back and let the words flow over them . . . to just listen?" people sometimes ask about the read-aloud. But I have to admit that I don't really see the read-aloud in this dreamy, sleepy sort of way. Too often children consider the read-aloud as a time to doze, dream, fiddle, and snack. I see read-aloud as the heart of our reading instruction time, and I want kids' full attention to be on what we do together. (Calkins 2001, p. 63)

Read-aloud is at the heart of your reading instruction when you adhere to the attitude that it is a critical component of a balanced or comprehensive literacy program, and not an optional activity (Routman 2000, pp. 14–15). Do not be tempted to do away with read-aloud in an attempt to pare away every "nonessential" activity and pack the school day full of "score-raising work," despite the increased pressure you feel from administrators, parents, and politicians to raise the test scores of your students. My response to these outside pressures has been to take a hard look at all the times during the school day designed to encourage lifelong learning, such as read-aloud, and reading and writing workshops, and find ways to make sure they pay off in the short term (test scores) as well as the long term (lifelong readers and writers).

Read-aloud is at the heart of your reading instruction when you recognize it as a time when you will do your best teaching; when you will use all the phases of the Apprenticeship Model—not just modeling, but also shared and guided learning. I discovered when I applied the Apprenticeship Model to my teaching that if those middle phases are skipped, the students are less likely to be successful in the independent practice of what was taught. During read-aloud, shared learning is most evident in whole-class discussions. The teacher lends support as students take the risk to express themselves in public, try to make their ideas coherent, learn to contribute to the thread of thought in the discussion rather than just throwing out random thoughts, and remember to participate in the discussion in a mannerly and democratic way. When students take the opportunity or are given the opportunity to talk in small groups about the read-aloud, guided learning is taking place. The teacher is usually available, if needed, to referee, or redirect, or simply listen in as students work together to construct meaning and ideas about the read-aloud. These conversations are at their best when they happen spontaneously between students—in the line waiting to leave for lunch, whispered during the read-aloud, or on the bus trip home from school. To make sure spontaneous conversations about the read-aloud happen, the teacher can make time for students to talk in pairs or small groups before, during, or after read-aloud. Finally, you should make it clear to your students that read-aloud is a teaching and learning time, and that you expect not only their participation but also evidence in their own reading lives that they are applying what they learn.

Read-aloud is at the heart of your reading instruction when it serves as a mirror that reflects the teaching you do during reading workshop. If you are studying characters in reading workshop, it is natural to focus on the characters during read-aloud. If your students are learning to make text-to-text, text-to-self, and text-to-world connections in reading workshop, you'll want to find such connections during read-aloud. Whatever you are teaching in reading workshop—use of sticky notes, summarizing, creating text sets, determining importance, and so on—can be reflected and reinforced during read-aloud.

Read-aloud can be as much at the heart of reading instruction in a middle school classroom as it is in an elementary school classroom. A day divided into discrete forty-four-minute periods might make it difficult or impossible to read aloud a novel to your students, but read-aloud at the middle school level can be woven into the reading instruction. Sixth-grade teacher Carol Wiltse reads something aloud to her students every day—every class, every period. Sometimes it is simply a newspaper article that connects with what her classes have been studying. Other times it is a picture book that helps "to get a point across in a different way . . . not out of a textbook." Many times she reads aloud from the novel her students are studying as they follow along—read-aloud from the "shared reading" end of the spectrum. She and her reading colleagues have even encouraged read-aloud across the middle school curriculum by sharing picture book titles that the social studies, math, and science teachers can use with their units.

Read-aloud is at the heart of your reading instruction when you value the teaching you do during read-aloud enough to assess your students' learning of what you've taught. Because read-aloud is an informal teaching time, the best assessment tools are also informal: observation, anecdotal records, and simple open-ended surveys and questions. Remember, assessment doesn't have to mean grading. Students don't have to use a pencil for you to assess their learning. Trees do not need to be sacrificed to make ditto packets for students to answer questions about read-aloud. In the same way that your best teaching is wrapped in the enjoyment of read-aloud, make sure that your assessment enhances rather than detracts from it.

Read-aloud is at the heart of your reading instruction because of all the authentic thinking skills it promotes: as you read to them, students practice the fundamental skill of listening intently, they connect what they know to new information and ideas, they are thinking actively and critically, and they are creating meaning. During read-aloud, your students are engaged in habits of the mind that will serve them well all through their life of learning and listening and thinking.

Read-aloud is the heart of your reading instruction when it is a time that you love and that your students love. Before you use read-aloud for teaching (and your students "learn without trying"), it must be a time your students enjoy. When I ask my classes at the end of each year what their favorite thing about read-aloud was, the most common responses are that it was relaxing, quiet, calm, comforting, and a break. I celebrate their responses as evidence of the success of my teaching during read-aloud. I had wrapped some of my most vigorous teaching of high-level reading concepts in the comfort of read-aloud, and although the comfort remained my students' favorite part, other answers revealed that my teaching was not lost. If your students begin to dread read-aloud, rather than beg for more, it has moved away from the heart of your reading instruction. Teach less so they can learn more. If you make read-aloud a time when you teach out of your love for stories and books and the escape to a "parallel universe," and you make it a time when students can learn with enjoyment and "without trying," then read-aloud will be the heart of your reading instruction, because you and your students will love it.

Set the Tone for Read-Aloud

Along with personal and professional philosophical roles for a teacher who wants to make read-aloud more of a teaching time, several other practical roles are important on a day-to-day basis. One of the first to consider is the tone of read-aloud.

I practice the art of an entertaining read-aloud by reading with dramatic expression, changing my voice (wherever possible) for different characters, and using facial expressions. My students most often sit at their desks during read-aloud, and I move throughout the classroom as I read, sometimes mirroring the movement in the story, but most times just to give my students a change in the direction of their focus and to monitor attentiveness. I monitor attentiveness because while I'm practicing the art of reading aloud well, I expect them to be practicing the art of listening well. I expect them to not be fiddling with pencils or writing notes or doodling with their markers or completing other work while I read aloud. It's hard, but we practice from the very first read-aloud. I usually choose shorter novels at the beginning of the year to mirror the kind of reading I expect them to do, but the added benefit is that shorter books and chapters help them build the listening stamina they need so that later in the year when the schedule allows, I can read aloud and they can listen—happily and totally engaged—for an hour or more.

I have had at least one memorable flop, which happened when I neglected to attend to the tone on a day-to-day or at least a book-to-book basis. The newest issue of *Muse* magazine, published by the Smithsonian Institution, contained several articles on the theme of risk-taking that I thought the students would enjoy. We had just finished a short chapter book and it had been several read-alouds since we had done nonfiction, so the timing was perfect for the *Muse* articles. At read-aloud time, I invited the class to the meeting area so that it would be easier to see the illustrations and sidebar graphics in that day's article. Looking at the cover of the magazine opened our discussion of how our perceptions of risk and danger cause us to fear or not to fear. The cover showed a large shark with its gigantic mouth wide open. We talked about how our perception of sharks might cause us to think it was a picture of a scary, dangerous animal, when in fact, it was a picture of a whale shark, a filter-feeding plankton eater without any teeth. As I read the article, what began as enthusiastic interaction with the ideas in the article became side conversations between friends sitting together on the floor, and then giggly silliness. We were out of time for read-aloud, and I was out of patience with my class. I sent them back to their seats, grumbling to myself that I had tried to share with them an interesting article full of serious ideas that I wanted them to think critically about so that the other articles in the magazine would make more sense, and look what I got. The next day I was out of the classroom for a meeting. I left instructions with my substitute to read the *Muse* article about the Mallory expedition on Mount Everest, but I told her to keep the students in their seats since they had been so squirrelly for me the previous day. I was still cranky about their behavior during read-aloud when I returned to school the following day. I had my parent volunteers track down an article in an earlier *Muse* about Shackleton's expedition to Antarctica that I thought might connect well with the other two articles on risk and danger. "We'll keep practicing this until they get it right!" I thought to myself.

And then I practically slapped my forehead at my own stupidity. Of course we need to keep practicing! Read-aloud had not failed that day because of what my students had done; it had failed because of what I had *not* done. I had not properly set the tone. I knew what my goal was—to share with them an interesting article full of serious ideas that I wanted them to think about critically so that the other articles in the magazine would make more sense—but I had failed to share those goals with my students.

At the beginning of read-aloud, before I read the Shackleton article, we talked about the Mallory expedition and how it fit with (the little they remembered of) the first article about risk and danger. I told them that I would read an article about an expedition to Antarctica and that I wanted them to pay close attention to all the connections they could make between the Antarctic expedition and the Mount Everest expedition. Although I knew I wanted to work on appropriate behavior when we had read-aloud in the meeting area, I started the article with them at their seats. Then I feigned frustration at how long it would take to bring the magazine around to every table so they could see the pictures, and wondered aloud, "It would be so much more efficient to read this to you in the meeting area where you are all close and can all see the pictures at the same time. Shall we try that? When you come to the meeting area, I want you to think about who you sit by. You need to be able to be serious and listen carefully so you can hear all the text-to-text connections between this article and the one about the Mallory expedition."

Setting the tone for the read-aloud made all the difference in the world. My students knew the purpose of the read-aloud, and my goals for their participation. They listened carefully, made connections, asked questions about vocabulary, and learned about an amazing man who led an amazing expedition from which every man returned alive. "Wow! That's like *Survivor*, except for real instead of for money!" John exclaimed.

The Art of Teaching During Read-Aloud

When you have placed read-aloud at the heart of your reading instruction and set the tone for a read-aloud that will be a time of learning, as well as enjoyment, your next role is to make sure that some of your best teaching takes place during that time.

Teaching is an art, and the best teachers are highly creative. Diane Ackerman once taught a college course on creativity in the arts and sciences. In class, she and the students identified some elements essential to creativity. When you consider your own best teaching, or the teaching of those who serve as role models for you, you can see how most, if not all, of these elements apply to the art of teaching:

> . . . risk, perseverance, novel problem solving, disciplined spontaneity, the need to make exterior one's inner universe, openness to experience, luck, genetics, a willingness to react against the status quo, delight, mastery, the ability to live not only one's own life but also the life of one's time, childlike innocence guided by the sophistication of an adult, resourcefulness, a sense of spirituality, a mind of large general knowledge fascinated by particulars, passion, the useful application of obsession, a sacred place (abstract or physical), among many others. (Ackerman 2001, p. 36)

The fourth item on Ackerman's list, disciplined spontaneity, is definitely necessary for good teaching. Even if your teaching is well planned, it is not scripted. Teaching is a daily exercise in impromptu speaking and thinking. Your best teaching is done spontaneously, based on a subconscious blend of all you've learned, who you are, who your students are, and what your students need at that moment. A good teacher is always alert for "the teachable moment." Knowing what to do with a teachable moment—knowing how to be productive in our spontaneity—requires a deep knowledge of the district graded course of study, the state standards, and the best thinking of colleagues and professional writers.

Spontaneity is one of read-aloud's particular joys. I have never met a teacher who wrote lesson plans for read-aloud. However, if read-aloud is to be used as a teaching time, rather than simply an entertaining time used to calm students after a recess, a teacher must be disciplined. Disciplined in carefully choosing what books to read aloud when, and knowing how and why the read-aloud fits with all the rest of one's reading instruction. Disciplined in the wealth of knowledge of outcomes, standards, reading strategies, connections, and literary conventions that a good teacher sorts and sifts in the back of her mind at every moment during the read-aloud.

Teach Lightly During Read-Aloud

Consider everything you know as a reader to be the toolbox that you bring to your teaching during read-aloud. As a reader, you know that first and foremost, read-aloud should be a time of enjoyment for both the reader and the listeners. Enjoyment is the entire top layer in your toolbox. Lift up the layer of enjoyment and you find compartments that hold everything you know about books and authors, reading skills and strategies, objectives and outcomes, and standards. Everything you know about your students fills the rest of the toolbox: their personal reading histories, your class's reading history, their ages and abilities, and their cultures and families.

As you read aloud, keep this toolbox open and ready. The teacher in you will probably want to write lesson plans and plan activities for read-aloud. The teacher in you will probably need to know before you read the book what skills and strategies you will be teaching on what page or in what chapter. Make the teacher in you sit in the corner during read-aloud. Follow your knowledge, the book, and your students when you choose what to teach and what not to teach. Be flexible and spontaneous. Give yourself permission to write in your lesson plans at the end of the day what you *did* teach rather than trying to decide a week or a day in advance what you *will* teach during read-aloud. Keep a record, rather than trying to make a map.

Even though the teacher in you is pouting from the corner, she knows in her heart that this is the best arrangement. When you let your instruction follow the interests, questions, and needs of your students, you cannot plan the direction it will go. Whether your teaching leads or follows during read-aloud, there *will* be teaching. The difference will be in the richness of the learning. For example, you come to the end of a chapter. You know that the ability to do an organized, detailed retelling or a concise summary are skills that take lots of time and all kinds of practice. You lead with your teaching when you say, "Let's work together to retell that chapter." The results will be a group retelling. With the same eventual outcome of a group retelling in mind, you would follow your students by asking, "What happened in this chapter?" This question may or may not result immediately in a retelling. Instead, you might find out that some or many of the students were actually confused about what happened in the chapter. You might gain insight into how they are connecting the events of this chapter with the rest of the book. They might begin making predictions, connections, or comparisons. At this point, you might redirect the students toward a retelling, or you might choose to abandon your goal of a retelling to work on a more immediate and interesting problem or skill or question. When you follow your students, you must be flexible with your teaching, but you can be confident they will provide you with numerous opportune directions for your teaching.

Whether your teaching leads or follows, you must teach lightly during read-aloud. Never forget that the main goal of read-aloud is the enjoyment of a great book. Your quick interjections during the read-aloud that clarify vocabulary, highlight a reading skill or strategy, invite quick predictions, and so on, should barely interrupt the flow of the story. Discussions can add to the enjoyment of the book, as well as being fun on their own. Sometimes students happily spend most of a read-aloud time talking about the book rather than listening to it—most often when they have initiated the discussion, not you. My rule of thumb with discussion is to honor all the voices and to let it follow a thread of thought not just until someone grows impatient and says, "Can we just get back to the book and read now?" but until everyone who wants to contribute has done so.

Every read-aloud session does not have to include interjected teaching or discussion. Days can go by in which read-aloud is entirely reading and listening. On days like that, you are still teaching during read-aloud.

It is teaching with your lightest touch—the kind where you simply provide the opportunity to learn. On those days, your students will be learning to maintain focused listening, visualize the story in their mind, and sustain and develop their comprehension. They will be working in the independent phase of the Apprenticeship Model to "construct a network of techniques for themselves" (Fountas and Pinnell 2001, p. 323).

You Can't Buy Your Read-Aloud at the Store

The teacher is the most important ingredient in the read-aloud. A high-quality read-aloud depends on a skilled and creative teacher who is a reader knowledgeable about books and authors, reading skills and strategies. It is critical for the teacher to know her students well and to tailor the teaching to those particular students.

Because the success of read-aloud depends on a particular teacher with a particular group of students sharing a particular book, there is no way to script a teacher's edition for a read-aloud. Nor would it be possible to prepackage activities and reproducibles for a read-aloud. Such store-bought teaching would be as shallow as a paint-by-number painting and as bland as a TV dinner. It would narrowly limit the read-aloud, which has as its primary feature the ability to expand the thinking of students and the teaching of a talented teacher.

You can't buy a premade read-aloud at the store. Like fine art or fine cooking, you begin with the outcome as a vision in your mind—a beautiful painting, a delicious meal, a read-aloud that is an elegant blend of story and conversation, teaching and learning. Like the outcomes of fine art or fine cooking, the ultimate read-aloud gives pleasure, no matter what else it does. To make your art, your meal, or your read-aloud, you gather the best materials and combine them in traditional and innovative ways. It takes time and focused study and multiple attempts before you ever get close to the creation of your original vision, and the process of creation is as satisfying as the elusive perfect outcome. You can't buy that in a store.

2

Choosing Books

In August, before school started, I sat down on the floor in front of my picture-book collection with a plastic shoe box. I was going to do what I'd read about in many professional books: pick out a core set of picture books that we would return to over and over again in reading and writing workshops. I filled the box before I got to the second shelf of books. Clearly, this would be much harder than I had originally thought. As I looked over my first choices, I noticed that several categories seemed to be emerging. There were certain authors I wanted to make sure my students knew, such as

Cynthia Rylant. There were books that communicated values I wanted to share with my students, such as *The Table Where the Rich People Sit* by Byrd Baylor and *Yo? Yes!* by Chris Raschka. I chose some books with writing workshop in mind, because of their unique format, such as *Mouse Tale/Giant Story* by Annegert Fuschuber. I knew for sure that one of my students would be coming to me with an "I hate school—you can't tell me what to do" kind of attitude, and that most fourth graders like to at least play around with the idea of defying authority, being, as they are, on the brink of young adulthood, when they'll finally be able to start being their own authority. So I chose *The Secret Knowledge of Grown-ups* by David Wisniewski to give us the opportunity to laugh together at grown-ups and at the rules they impose on children.

I finally winnowed my choices down to one shoe box full. These, I decided, would be my read-alouds for the first week of school. Then I would move on to short chapter books that I could finish reading aloud in a week or less, to mirror the kinds of reading choices I was asking my students to make for the first three weeks (as Lucy Calkins suggests in *The Art of Teaching Reading*)—quick reads, from a variety of genres, at or slightly below the student's reading level, to develop reading stamina and fluency.

I didn't get even halfway through the box in the first four days of school. As usual, the classroom that I had created in my mind for the sake of imagining how those first lessons would go barely matched the real class that came in and sat down on the first day. We wound up reading, discussing, and laughing about *The Secret Knowledge of Grown-ups* for two of the first four days of school. It didn't help that I had discovered the brand new sequel, *The Secret Knowledge of Grown-ups: The Second File*, just before school started. When I was finished reading *The Secret Knowledge of Grown-ups*, I thought I would just mention *The Second File* and move on to the next read-aloud book. After the response to the first book, however, I realized that if I did that, a riot would probably ensue over who would get to read *The Second File* first, and that the waiting list would mean some students might have to wait months before they got their hands on it. So instead of starting a short chapter book on Monday of the second week of school, we spent two more days reading *The Second File*.

There were unplanned benefits that came from doing that. By the sixth day of the school year we were already comparing two books by the same author and analyzing them to decide which we thought was better. From the outset, I told the class that I thought *The Second File* was much funnier than the first, and that David Wisniewski did a much better job making the logs for the discovery of each file funnier. Here's what else happened in the first six days of school: my class learned that it's okay to disagree with me. The more obvious, slapstick humor of *The Secret Knowledge of Grown-ups* worked better for them. The plays on words and the jokes that take more than nine years of background experience to understand made *The Second File* my choice. We did agree that Wisniewski made the logs funnier in *The Second File*.

That was a glimpse into the selection process I used for the first read-alouds of the school year. Every book after that had its own unique selection process. How do you choose books for your read-aloud? Out of all the great chapter, nonfiction, poetry, and picture books, which do you choose? It helps to know lots of books. It's not a bad thing to have so many old friends on your shelf that it pains you to make one shoe box full of choices. If all you know is one shoe box full, then you've got enough to start with while you begin to read widely and find more favorites.

Using High-Quality Literature in the Read-Aloud

An educated guess might be that starting with 8-year-olds—when teachers begin to read longer, continuous stories to boys and girls—an average of some six to ten books are read aloud during the year. This means that for the next four years, when children are reaching the peak of their interest in reading, they may hear no more than forty or so books read by their teachers! Today when there are more than ninety thousand children's books in print, read-aloud choices must be selected with care in terms of their relevance for students and the quality of their writing. (Huck, Hepler, and Hickman 1987, p. 646)

The most important starting point when choosing books for read-aloud is high-quality literature. Read-aloud is your chance to introduce your students to the award winners, to the newest books, to the classics. The Internet makes it easier than ever to choose books for your classroom. "The Children's Literature Web Guide" (http://www.ucalgary.ca/

~dkbrown/) lists the winners of twenty-one different U.S. children's book awards, as well as ten U.S. regional awards. You can follow links that take you to sites that recommend books for all kinds of reasons. As the site says, "Everyone has an opinion." You can find lists of best books, banned books, and books about specific subjects. There are also links to children's author sites and links to many other resources for teachers and readers.

"Carol Hurst's Children's Literature Site" (http://www.carolhurst .com) has a myriad of ways to find books—by title, author, grade level, curriculum area, and "other subjects and themes in children's literature." You can even sign up for a free electronic children's literature newsletter produced by Hurst.

For quick reviews of books grouped in very practical ways, "BookHive: Your Guide to Children's Literature," (http://bookhive.org), a site produced by the Public Library of Charlotte and Mecklenburg County, North Carolina, with reviews written by children's librarians in their system, is an excellent resource. You can search their site by author, title, illustrator, book audience (age level), genre, and number of pages. When you click on a genre link, you can narrow your search by designating the age level within that genre. The books on this site are not always the newest, but sometimes it's good to be reminded of old favorites. Befitting a site produced by librarians, it might remind you of a leisurely walk through the aisles of the children's section of your library, but you can scan the titles here without the stiff neck you get from turning your head to read titles on book spines! I was browsing this site during winter break and ran across *Be a Perfect Person in Just Three Days* by Stephen Manes. This used to be my favorite first book of the school year, but it would also be a perfect quick read for the first week of the new year as we wrote resolutions and set goals for ourselves. And there was *The Sign of the Beaver* by Elizabeth George Speare, a perfect book to recommend as a follow-up to *Weasel* by Cynthia DeFelice, the book we had finished right before break.

The larger, more comprehensive sites will be all the help you need with your book selections most of the time, but if you search deeply enough, you can also find specialized sites that give you the information you need for finding a particular book on a particular topic. For example, "Guide to Children's Literature and Disability" (http://www.kidsource .com/NICHCY/literature.html) contains a bibliography of children's literature categorized by disability.

There are also outstanding print resources that review and discuss children's literature. If you pick only one, browse *The Hornbook* for reviews of the newest and best children's books. Other magazines and journals that are helpful include *Book Links*, the *New Advocate*, and *Booklist*.

As you consider all of the highest-quality children's books, you might choose to read aloud a book because it is an award-winning work of children's literature. Don't forget to look beyond the Newbery and Caldecott winners to consider books such as Ralph Fletcher's *Uncle Daddy*, which is a Christopher Award winner, a book that "affirms the highest values of the human spirit" (www.ucalgary.ca/~dkbrown/).

Another reason to choose a book might be that you want your students to get acquainted with one of the best children's authors. You might pick *Hatchet* or *Mr. Tucket* to introduce your students to Gary Paulsen, *Baby* to introduce them to Patricia MacLachlan, or *The Tarantula in My Purse* to introduce them to Jean Craighead George.

Sometimes you pick a read-aloud to introduce your students to a new genre. *The Clock* by the Collier brothers could begin a study of historical fiction, Betsy Byars's *The Moon and I* a study of autobiographies, or *The Green Book* by Jill Paton Walsh a study of science fiction.

Sometimes it is fun to select a read-aloud with a unique format that will stretch your students' ideas of what a book can be, what a genre can be, or how genres can blend. One of my favorites is *Mouse Tale/Giant Story* (Fuschuber), a picture book that contains two stories, and two front covers. The book can be read from either end, and the stories dovetail in the center spread. Children love discovering familiar fairy-tale and nursery-rhyme characters in new stories. Middle grade students are not too old for Alma Flor Ada's *Dear Peter Rabbit* books, David Weisner's Caldecott-winning *The Three Pigs*, or the puns in Janet Stevens's *And the Dish Ran Away with the Spoon*. In *Summer Reading Is Killing Me!*, Jon Scieszka's literary allusions are more sophisticated, and include characters and situations from children's novels, as well as picture books, fairy tales, and nursery rhymes.

Several years ago, I chose a read-aloud because it and its sequels were (are) a current worldwide literary phenomenon in which I wanted my students to participate. I read *Harry Potter and the Sorcerer's Stone* by J. K. Rowling to my fourth graders when there were only two books in the series and before the first movie was released. Many of my students had not yet read Harry Potter, most were excited to have the chance to hear it, and none of their parents had expressed any reservations about their children hearing it. What a difference a few years and a movie release make. I surveyed my students at the beginning of the 2001–2002 school year and found only a couple of Harry Potter fans. Most claimed to have already read all four of the books. Nearly all of them saw the movie when it came out. When I considered those factors, plus the limited number of books I could read aloud in any given year, I could not justify the time I would spend reading Harry Potter.

Know Your Students

The next important consideration in choosing a book for your read-aloud is your students. Every year, a unique community of distinct individuals fills your classroom. Because you are the constant in the classroom each year, you might be tempted to use the same read-alouds with the same units, in the same order every year because *you* know them and *you* love them. Do the math. You are outnumbered by twenty or thirty to one. Who your students are should play a huge part in the books you choose to read to them. With your students in mind, you might choose a book because it is just right for their age or developmental stage. Third-grade teacher Karen Terlecky reads the Junie B. Jones series at the beginning of the year. At that point, her students are only two years out of kindergarten, and they can relate to Junie's bossy, self-centered approach to life. Later, she reads another book by Barbara Park, *Skinnybones*, because the humor is so perfect for third graders. On the other hand, you might choose *not* to read a book because of your students' age or developmental stage. No matter how much I love the book, I personally would not read Lois Lowry's *The Giver* to fourth- or even fifth-grade students. I would save that book for middle school, when students have more personal maturity (to think about and understand "stirrings" and "releases") and more maturity as readers (to come up with a plausible theory about the end).

As you consider your students as a factor in the choice of a read-aloud, you might choose a book because it features characters who are in the same grade as your students. *Tales of a Fourth Grade Nothing* by Judy Blume obviously would work in fourth grade, and *Frindle* by Andrew Clements features a fifth-grade main character.

As the school year progresses, you learn more and more about your students as readers. Each student continues to develop his own personal reading history, and your class develops a group reading history, fueled by and somewhat controlled by peer recommendations, your recommendations, and the collection of books in your classroom and your school. Knowing your students as readers, you might choose a book because the author or the series is popular in your classroom. Sometimes you can choose to read aloud what your least-able readers are reading, because you want to validate the book choices of all the readers in your classroom, not just the most able, and sometimes the book you choose might build on or extend your students' understanding of an author, a type of character, a genre, or a historical period.

You also know your students as unique human beings. You learn about all the cultures to which each of them belongs: gender, family, ethnic, religious, neighborhood, friendship group, and so on. When a child sees himself in the book that is being read aloud, he receives a powerful validation. I see this in the faces of my African American students when I read *The Watsons Go to Birmingham—1963* by Christopher Paul Curtis, and in the faces of my Muslim children when I read *Ramadan* by Suhaib Hamid Ghazi. I try hard to alternate books with girls as main characters with books that have boys as main characters. Although gender equity is important to me, I didn't realize the students paid much attention to it in terms of book characters until one girl commented after we finished *Weasel*, "I hope the next book has a girl for the main character." Finally, every child has also had unique life experiences, both positive (travel, for example) and negative (such as divorce).

Knowing your students as complicated, unique people, you might choose a book in hopes that it will expand or confirm their understanding of the range of responses to all kinds of life events. Nuclear and extended family relationships, the death of a sibling, and personal integrity are all topics that can be explored with *Fig Pudding* by Ralph Fletcher. *On My Honor* by Marion Dane Bauer deals with peer pressure and the death of a friend. In *Just Juice* by Karen Hesse, poverty and illiteracy are issues.

Consider Your Curriculum and Reading Objectives

Finally, after taking into consideration the highest-quality children's literature and the particular needs and interests of your students, you might choose a book for read-aloud that will provide you with a predetermined teaching opportunity. This can be the last consideration when choosing a book for read-aloud. Your best teaching is intuitive, spontaneous, and responsive to a great piece of literature and to your students' conversations about it. Your best teaching follows the book and your students. With every book you read aloud, during the course of the reading and the discussions you and your students have, you will introduce or reinforce numerous objectives and/or standards without ever planning to do so.

When you let your teaching lead by choosing a book with some particular teaching point in mind, don't ignore the opportunities to follow the book and your students in directions you didn't originally choose. For example, last year when I chose to read aloud *Holes* by Louis Sachar, I chose it, first of all, because it's a great piece of literature, but I also chose it because of the way the story moves back and forth between the past and the present. I wanted my students to learn to recognize all of the clues an author gives so that the reader doesn't get lost in the back and forth. This was a skill or strategy that I knew would serve them well as they moved into more and more complex books. We did a lot of work on the temporal setting of the story, but the most memorable teaching moment was an unplanned discussion of symbolism that resulted in students finding further examples of symbolism in *Holes* as well as in their independent reading books. Stay open to every teaching opportunity, even if you choose a book for read-aloud because it will introduce or reinforce a certain reading skill or strategy; because it fits in with your content curriculum in social studies, science, or mathematics; because it has a unique style of writing that you will spotlight in writing workshop; because it will mirror the kind of reading you are asking your students to do in reading workshop; because it has a message or value you want to communicate or reinforce; or because you think it will spark lively discussion.

Finding New Read-Alouds

Keep Your Eyes Open When You Read

No matter what I'm reading, I am always on the lookout for a new read-aloud. Naturally, every children's book I read is under consideration. As I read, I imagine how the book would sound read out loud, whether the pacing of the story and the language would be good for listening, and what the reaction of my students might be. When I read Jerry Spinelli's *Wringer* for the first time, I imagined the passionate discussions we would have. Kate DiCamillo's *Because of Winn-Dixie* introduced me to a lovable new dog character I had to share with my class. After I heard *The Three Little Pigs and the Fox* by William Hooks read aloud in a wonderful, slow, Appalachian drawl, I knew I would have to read it aloud so that I, too, could have that accent, at least temporarily.

You can find just the right books if you are always alert to possibilities. When Carol Wiltse, a sixth-grade teacher, was browsing the books for sale at the Dublin Literacy Conference in Ohio, she spotted the book *If You Lived 100 Years Ago* by Ann McGovern. Carol remembered how hard it had been for her students to imagine what their great-grandmothers might have done. Here was the perfect book in the perfect format—questions and short, one-page answers with fun illustrations.

Not every read-aloud has to be a book. Much of the nonfiction I read aloud is in the form of newspaper or magazine articles. When my students were involved in creating their own cities, I read aloud a *USA Today* article that I found about the annual national Future City competition. On a clear night after book club, I pointed out the constellation Orion to prove that my Halloween costume could actually be found in the night sky. Several days later in the astronomy column of the *Sunday Columbus* (Ohio) *Dispatch* I found an article to read aloud about Orion that included a Native American myth to explain how Orion came to be in the night sky. Another newspaper article I found was interesting not so much because of how the topic connected to something that was going on in my class, but because of the way it was written. If you had read only the headline and the first few paragraphs, you would have thought it was an article confirming that dinosaurs were feathered and that birds evolved from dinosaurs. Halfway through the article, the point of view shifted and the second half refuted the dinosaur-bird connection. This one short article provided a powerful lesson on the need to read a piece all the way through before deciding what it is about.

Preview Every Book All the Way Through Before You Read It Aloud

Never read aloud a book, an article, or even a poem unless you have read it all the way through first. Don't take *anyone's* advice on a great read-aloud without reading the book yourself. Not even your best friend's. Not even mine. You need to read *James and the Giant Peach* (Dahl) and decide for yourself what you will say when the centipede starts swearing. You need to read *Weasel* (DeFelice) and decide if Ezra getting his tongue cut out is too violent for you or for your students. You need to decide whether you can lead discussions about killing pigeons that are sure to occur if you read *Wringer* (Spinelli). You have to be prepared for any character's death so that you won't cry, or so that you'll have the tissue box close at hand, or so that you can ask a student to read that page for you.

If you've read the text first, you will be better able to lead discussions. You will know when a good place to stop would be—either for a cliffhanger or for closure. You will have worked out the way to say the difficult names, and you will have investigated any new vocabulary. You will have made connections to other texts, to yourself, to your students, and to the world. Instead of just reading the text to your students, you will be prepared to lead them through it, teaching lightly as you go.

ᘒ 3 ᘒ

Building Classroom Community

The most important learning that occurs at the beginning of each school year is not tied to any formal curriculum content. The initial work that teachers and students do to create their classroom community is the most important work they will do together all year. The first weeks of school are what make the middle weeks productive and the last weeks powerful.

Beginning the school year with a new class is a dance of expectations, negotiations, and associations. Sometimes teachers and students waltz formally as the boundaries of the classroom community are defined.

Other times are more like jazz improvisation. And there are times when the teacher must step aside and let the students become the choreographers of the classroom community.

Read-aloud can be an essential element in creating a basic classroom community as well as a community of readers. The books we choose for read-aloud and the conversations that surround our read-alouds help us build the relationships that are important in any community. The rituals we create around read-aloud put it at the center of our reading instruction and elevate its status in our classroom community of readers. The big topics we address with our read-alouds are indicative of the levels of trust and honesty we have developed in our classroom community.

Relationships

The first relationship that read-aloud nurtures is a selfish one—the teacher's relationship with books. "I'm not reading to them because it's good for them; I'm reading to them because it's good for me" (Ray 1999, p. 80). If you are a reader, preparing for read-aloud will be a natural extension of your love of books and reading. You will read with your ear tuned for the book that would be perfect to listen to, that would be ideal for this particular class, that would spark intense discussions. For the teacher who is a reader, read-aloud time satisfies the desire to talk about and share great books. Over and over again, when I ask teachers who are readers, "What do you love most about read-aloud?" they talk about sharing great books, the discussions those books start, and the joy of getting even one student in their class hooked on reading because of the read-aloud.

More important, read-aloud nurtures a unique relationship between a teacher and her students. During read-aloud, you become more like a parent and less like a teacher. Your voice and the story it carries to the children provide the same calming comfort a parent's voice does during a bedtime read-aloud. During read-aloud, you do not use your teacher voice: your evaluating work and behavior voice, your refereeing disagreements voice, your authority voice, your explaining voice. During read-aloud, you use your voice to make a story come to life for your students. Each teacher uses her voice during read-aloud in an individual way. Some go so far as to create a different voice for each character. We all see read-aloud as somewhat of a performance, and use a blend of expression and inflection in our voice, animated facial expressions, and even movement while reading. One thing is true for all of us: we know our students love the way we read to them. After a substitute they complain, "She didn't read it right!" I have had classes beg me to reread the part the substitute read, and one class forbade me to let a substitute read from the read-aloud. They decided they would rather go without read-aloud than hear it "wrong." Never underestimate the significance of your voice during read-aloud, and the connection it forges between you and your students.

Read-aloud also provides the opportunity for teachers and students to build a common relationship with books. Read-aloud is a rare time when you and your students do something together, more like equals than at any other time during the day. You laugh together during the funny parts, cry together during the sad parts, help each other understand the confusing parts, and sigh together at the endings. Your read-aloud books and their language, characters, and situations become the common currency in your classroom. Your read-aloud books become the common referent. Everyone hasn't seen the same movies or TV shows, everyone hasn't read the same books independently, everyone doesn't have the same supply of background experiences. But everyone in your room has heard the same read-alouds, and those books can function as the hitching post to which each reader in the classroom can tie ideas.

To begin building this web of relationships between you and your students and books, you have to make sure they fall as deeply in love with read-aloud as you have. It's not too hard. From the minute they walk into their new classroom, they'll see that it's a place where books are valued. In the first few days of school, when you carve out big chunks of time for all kinds of read-alouds, they'll understand the importance you assign to it. When they see that you can be trusted to pick books that they love, well, they're hooked.

It was the third day of school in my classroom, and the students were hungry for sustained sustained silent reading. They had been living for three days in a classroom filled with shelves, tubs, crates, and carts full of books. They were greeted on the first day of school by Captain Underpants's underpants on the chalkboard (the paper version—a promotional) and Dav Pilkey's *Captain Underpants and the Wrath of the Wicked Wedgie Woman*, along with the two newest Magic Tree House books on the chalk tray. We had started organizing our district-provided grade-level classroom library, so they had seen and handled the picture books, poetry, chapter books, and nonfiction that would live in the bookshelves at the back of the room in the categories they created.

I loved it that they were hungry for SSR, but still I cast the tie-breaking vote to continue reading aloud *The Secret Knowledge of Grown-ups* (Wisniewski). As soon as we were settled in the meeting area, Darion set up Ethan to ask if they could choose whether to stay in the room for read-aloud or go out into the hall to read their own books. I smiled, knowing that in a few weeks they would all be as hungry for read-aloud as they were for SSR. I told the class that read-aloud in my room is not a choice or a kind of recess. It is part of their reading class, and during read-aloud they learn lots about reading and books and authors. Besides that, I let them know that I am fully aware that when students go out in the hall to read, reading is one of the last things that gets done.

Finally we could start read-aloud. A few students were close to my feet, eager to see all the details in the illustrations. Others were at the back, feigning indifference. As I read, the ones in the back pulled in closer and closer, getting up on their knees so they, too, could see. From all around the group, students called out to the text as I read. "I *never* comb *my* hair," Ethan said in defiance of the book's stated need to comb your hair so it won't grow back into your head. "That is *so* unbelievable," said Tsilat, with a delighted grin.

The inevitable happened. Sooner or later when you have children sitting in a group on the floor at the end of the day, someone is bound to fart. Someone did. Hysterical laughter ensued. I continued reading as a signal that the polite response to body noises is to ignore them, but Wisniewski seemed to have written his book as a script to go along with our read-aloud that day. In the next secret file, he gave us a perfect text-to-self connection when he revealed that the sound we had just heard can actually be that of a brain deflating because of nose picking. More hysterical laughter. This time I joined in. What else could I do?

"Will you read us *The Second File* tomorrow?" Becca begged.

At first it might have seemed to my students that read-aloud was just another item on the Teacher Agenda. After all, I voted for it over SSR, and I set the expectation for mandatory involvement. But once we got started, the class learned that they could trust me to pick books they would enjoy, that the teaching I wove in as I read was there to help them better understand and appreciate the story, that we would be able to laugh together during read-aloud, and that read-aloud in our classroom would be something to look forward to eagerly.

They were hooked.

Conversations

Helping children think about texts is as essential to the teaching of reading as it is to the whole of our lives, and the most powerful way to teach this kind of thinking is through book talks based on read-aloud books. We teach children to think with and between and against texts by helping them say aloud, in conversations with us and with others, the thoughts they will eventually be able to develop without the interaction of conversation. The great Russian psychologist Lev Vygotsky helped us realize that by giving our student practice in talking with others, we give them frames for thinking on their own. (Calkins 2001, p. 226)

The talk that surrounds the read-aloud is not something extra that is added to the reading of the book; the talk is as much a part of the read-aloud experience as the book. The conversation we have with our students about read-alouds teaches them much more than just skills and strategies for reading. Through conversation we can build and develop ideas together. Conversation is, by its very nature, a collaboration. Collaborating to build ideas also builds community.

A community of readers is a true democracy, with shared leadership. The chain of authority does not descend from the reader with the most skill and/or experience to the one with the least. It is an interconnected web of authority that builds on shared experience and knowledge. Allowing the read-aloud to be the center of the classroom reading community levels the playing field for readers of all abilities. Every child has access to the text through your voice, rather than through the print on the page. Every child can develop opinions and insights and speak them during read-aloud conversations, unburdened by pencil and paper.

The democracy of the read-aloud community was never more clear to me than when I was reading *Holes* (Sachar) to my fifth graders. We were at the point where Stanley is peeling an onion layer by layer, and Zero is revealing truths about himself to Stanley layer by layer. I had read

Holes at least three times before this, but never before had it occurred to me that this was a symbolic parallel. I stopped reading and wondered out loud whether Sachar had done that on purpose and would be proud of me for noticing it, or whether he would be amazed that I had found something in his book that even he didn't know was there. I wondered out loud if this parallel would show up again in the story. The class was intrigued by the fact that I'd found something new in a book I'd read several times before, by the idea of symbolic parallels, and by the notion that sometimes authors include parallels intentionally and sometimes unintentionally. I read on.

A day or two later, we came to a part where Stanley is eating another onion layer by layer, and sure enough, Zero reveals more truths about himself layer by layer. "There's that onion stuff again!" a student blurted out. Her keen listening and her enthusiastic contribution to the read-aloud conversation were remarkable. Even more remarkable was the number of labels she had to shed to get to that moment. In that moment, she was not learning disabled, time intensive, or difficult. She was an equal participant in the read-aloud and the conversation that surrounded it. She was the one who continued for the rest of the year's read-alouds to notice and point out symbolism of action and parallels of plot—known for the rest of the year in our classroom as "that onion stuff."

Rituals

Rituals make an event memorable by lifting it up and setting it apart. Rituals build community by providing a common set of experiences. I have created rituals for bringing a class together on the first day of school and for sending them off on the last day of school, for welcoming a new student and saying good-bye to a classmate, and for our birthdays. It seemed natural to add rituals to our read-aloud.

The Read-Aloud Gallery

We have a gallery of read-alouds that hangs in our room. After each read-aloud, I draw a name out of a bucket and that child creates a twelve-by-eighteen-inch illustration of a favorite part of the book. This large picture is hung, along with a sentence strip with the title and author of

big pictur

the book, in chronological order around the classroom up high where the wall meets the ceiling. (In another classroom where wall space is at a premium, I have seen the gallery of read-alouds attached to the ceiling tiles.) While one child is making "the big picture," the others make a nine-by-twelve-inch picture of their favorite part, which is spiral-bound into a class book.

class book

The ritual of pausing at the end of each read-aloud to commit to paper our favorite parts and to make visible the pictures we saw in our minds during the story has had the side benefit of creating a time line of read-alouds. In past years, each read-aloud evaporated into thin air when the book ended. The titles and authors were never instantly available so we could refer to them during discussions, and at the end of the year, we could never remember all of our read-alouds, let alone the order in which they'd been read. I thought the gallery of read-alouds would just be pictures of all the read-alouds for that class. Little did I know that it would become a concrete history of the books we'd shared—a record of the building of our classroom reading community. When I looped from

FIGURE 3.1 Katie's *Walk Two Moons* by Sharon Creech

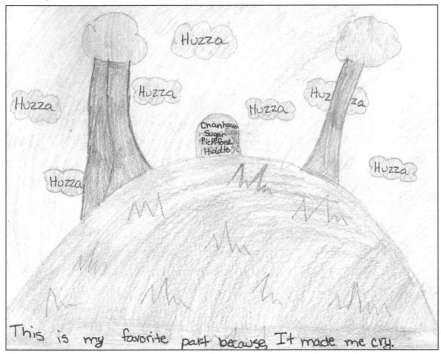

FIGURE 3.2 Jessica's Hera from *It's All Greek to Me* by Jon Scieszka

fourth to fifth grade with my class, Kaitlyn's picture of Josh stepping in the pudding at the end of *Fig Pudding* (Fletcher) was on the wall for two years, reminding us of where we had started.

The Birthday Read-Aloud

We refer to the read-aloud gallery every time there is a birthday in our class. One of the privileges of your birthday celebration in my room is to pick the birthday read-aloud, an idea I borrowed from Lucy Calkins's *Art of Teaching Reading* (2001). On the day we celebrate your birthday, you can pick any part from any previous read-aloud to revisit.

Never underestimate the power of a ritual. Never assume that something as simple as having the birthday child pick a favorite or memorable

pick any part from previous book

FIGURE 3.3 Garth's *Fig Pudding* by Ralph Fletcher

FIGURE 3.4 Amanda's *Weasel* by Cynthia DeFelice

part from a previous read-aloud will be anything but a rich and complex glimpse into a reader's mind. <u>Never ignore the power of returning to important books to reread a passage or a chapter.</u>

I was stunned nearly speechless by Ashley's choice for our very first birthday read-aloud. She wanted to go back to the part in *Weasel* (DeFelice) where Nathan and his father find Weasel dead and bury him. She didn't pick trivial; she didn't pick light; she went straight to the heart of the book, to the moral dilemma of doing the right thing, even—or especially—to one's enemies.

The chapter near the end of J. K. Rowlings's *Harry Potter and the Sorcerer's Stone* where Harry, Hermione, and Ron have to overcome the series of challenges that draw out the particular strength of each character was the most-requested birthday read-aloud of one class. Five more times after the original reading, the sorcerer's stone was saved from falling into the evil hands of Voldemort. Five more times, we saw that the hero could not have succeeded on his own—it was the talents and sacrifices of his friends that put him into position to do what he had the particular strengths and abilities to do. Five more times, the child was the hero, doing what adults could not or dared not do.

Near the end of that year, my biggest Harry Potter fan, Mathias, requested the chapter of *Harry Potter and the Sorcerer's Stone* where Harry, Ron, and Hermione attend their first potions class. After spending so much time with the climax of the book, this choice seemed odd, flat—until I read it. Mathias had picked the exact moment in the book when the plot turns.

Not every birthday read-aloud choice was deeply meaningful. Some were just for fun. We went back to the chapter about the cloud men in *James and the Giant Peach* (Dahl), to the part in *Holes* (Sachar) when Stanley drives the truck into the hole, and to the troll boogers in Harry Potter. On Rachel's birthday, I was in the middle of reading *Fig Pudding* (Fletcher) for the second time. Her birthday read-aloud choice was for me to keep reading *Fig Pudding*.

One year, Becca and Caitlyn shared a birthday. When it came time for them to pick their birthday read-alouds, they both went to the back of the classroom and looked up at the read-aloud gallery. Caitlyn picked first: *Dogzilla*, by Dav Pilkey. Becca wanted *Baloney (Henry P.)* by Jon Scieszka. At the time, I was disappointed. I wanted to be surprised by the part of a novel that so impressed a student that they wanted to hear that more than anything else on their birthday. Later, it occurred to me that I could be just as surprised that the girls picked two of our short read-alouds. That was the first year I included every book I read aloud in our gallery. The novels still get the big picture and sentence strip, but between each novel are the picture books and short books on pages from a notepad that looks like an open book. If I thought my read-alouds disappeared into thin air before we had the gallery, how much more true that was for all the picture books I read in between the novels. The picture books had never been chosen for rereading because they'd never been validated as part of the true read-aloud.

Lingering

In the same way that returning to a favorite or memorable or important part of a previous read-aloud can be an important ritual, so, too, is lingering with a read-aloud before going on to the next one. It's like putting the CD player on repeat so that you can listen to one song over and over again to memorize the lyrics. It's like the time spent making a scrapbook of the photos and memorabilia from your vacation. It's got the same feeling you have after dinner with friends, when everyone is full and happy and the conversation wanders down surprising paths and no one wants to be the one who says, "Well, I guess it's time . . ."

We have been known to stay with a book for a week or more after the read-aloud is technically finished. The power of lingering with the book was made especially clear to me in the time we spent with *Walk Two Moons* by Sharon Creech, rereading and discussing, laughing again and crying again. In the past, when the read-aloud ended with the last words of the book, I read the ending of *Walk Two Moons* only once. The students had just one chance to experience the way Creech weaves all the loose ends of story strands into the final tapestry. This time, we went back to the ending over and over again. For probably the third time, I was reading the part when Sal's grandmother is in the hospital and Sal takes the car and goes down the mountain to Lewiston to her mother's grave. When I read the line "I peered over the rail, looking for the bus that I knew was still somewhere down there on the side of the mountain, but I couldn't see it," Mark's hand shot up and he said, "Wait! I have a question. Does she already know that her mother is dead?"

As we had read the book, we were constantly monitoring Creech's use of time. In parts of the book, Sal is telling Phoebe's story—in flashback—

to Gram and Gramps on the trip to Idaho. But the trip to Idaho is a story in and of itself. Then there are the flashbacks to before the trip and before Euclid, Ohio, to Bybanks, Kentucky. It's hard to keep track of, and especially hard to explain as your students are hearing *Walk Two Moons* for the first time—you don't want to give away twists of plot.

Now that we were revisiting the ending, however, we could look at that part in the context of the whole book. As we talked about Mark's question, it became clear that not only Mark, but *many* of the students had not realized that Sal knows all through the book that her mother is dead; she just cannot accept it until she sees her tombstone by the river under the singing tree. No matter how many times we had read it, this part still made Katie cry again.

I cried again, too.

Rituals for Beginning a Read-Aloud

I do not have any set rituals for beginning read-aloud in my classroom, but Joyce Zawaly's fourth-grade classroom has definite rituals for starting read-aloud time. Students take out their Book Lover's Notebook and arrange their chairs in a half circle at the front of the room, or in a circle in the center of the classroom (depending on how the classroom is arranged). Joyce always does read-aloud with the students gathered around her, rather than at their desks, because she likes to have them "up close and personal."

Joyce also starts every read-aloud in the same way. She and her students look at the book cover and make predictions. They decide whether or not to read the blurb on the back. They discuss what they know about the author, and if anyone has read other books by the author, they share. They study the dedication page, any special quotes, how the book is set up, and the table of contents, chapter titles, and illustrations, if the book has any. Often in the first session with a book, Joyce doesn't even read aloud. All the work they do with the book models what a good reader does before reading. Joyce has found that her students' comprehension is improved when the class spends time studying the book before she starts to read it aloud.

Third-grade teacher Karen Terlecky begins every read-aloud by having her students carefully study the book in the same ways Joyce does, but with one twist: she photocopies the front and back cover, and any other parts of the book, such as the table of contents and dedication, that will give her third graders information with which to make their first predictions about it. Each student keeps these copies in the section in their Book Lover's Binder titled "Read-Aloud." At the end of every read-aloud, Karen and her students look back at these copies—the first information they had about the book—and remember their first predictions, and reflect on how their thinking changed over the course of the read-aloud. Initially, Karen's reason for making these copies was solely for the pre- and post-read-aloud discussions and reflections. At midyear, she realized an added benefit: the children's binders contained a history of the year's read-alouds to have at their fingertips during discussions, for comparing and contrasting books, and for reference to titles and authors. It was another example of the hidden power of ritual.

Student Involvement in Choice

You pay only lip service to the idea of community if your students are never involved in the choice of the read-aloud. If you don't have a specific book in mind for the next read-aloud, offer your class several options and let them choose. If you have several books in mind, give a book talk on each and let your class decide the order in which you'll read them.

Your students' choices of read-alouds can be surprising. When I chose *Fig Pudding* as the first read-aloud in the fourth-grade year of my first grades 4–5 loop, I had no idea that this book would be a seminal event in the building of our classroom community. I had no idea that we would come to see it as the beginning of our class's read-aloud history. I picked it thinking it would work well because of the short-story quality of the chapters, the puzzle of the yidda yadda, and the inevitability that I would cry when Brad dies, thus modeling an authentic emotional response to a story. (I was bound to cry sooner or later during a read-aloud, so I figured I might as well get it over with early.) I started to get a hint of what *Fig Pudding* meant to the class early in the fifth-grade year, when one of the students first suggested that *Fig Pudding* should be the last read-aloud of the year, and of our two years together. All year long we discussed, debated, and finally decided on and looked forward to *Fig Pudding* as our final read-aloud together. It wasn't until late in the fifth-grade year, however, when I asked the class which read-aloud was our most memorable and which was the most important, that it became really clear to me what *Fig Pudding* had meant to them. When I chose *Fig Pudding*, I never would have believed it would be either the most memorable or the most important, but it was both to many of my students. It was memorable, the students said, because it was our first book together. We didn't know each other yet, but we laughed together and cried together and got to know each other through the book and our conversations about it. It was one of the three most important read-alouds, in Ashleigh's opinion, because "it brought us together." *Fig Pudding* remains an anchor in my relationship with one of those students. A year later, when she had moved on to sixth grade and middle school, Amanda brought me a flowering Christmas cactus for my birthday. In *Fig Pudding*, the Christmas cactus is a key symbol for the healing of Cliff's family. The Christmas cactus that now sits on my kitchen windowsill is a constant reminder of how important a book can be in the life of one child, and in the life of a class.

Stay open to suggestions from your students and talk openly about what you think makes a good read-aloud. Kyle really wanted me to read aloud the fourth Harry Potter, but after we estimated how much time it would take, he realized that a better use of that time would be to read several books rather than just one. Ashley perfectly timed her suggestion that we read *The Hour of the Olympics* by Mary Pope Osborne. We were between read-alouds and the Summer Olympics were beginning in Australia, so I was able to take her suggestion. I shared with the class my dilemma of trying to find just the right book with a strong female character for our next read-aloud. Becca suggested *Meet Addy* by Connie Porter so that we could read a book with a strong female character *and* one with an African American main character for Black History Month.

One year I got extra mileage from giving my students a voice in choosing the next read-aloud. I had my class practice persuasive writing for the Ohio Off-Year Proficiency Test by asking them to write me a letter convincing me that I should read aloud a certain book next. I promised them I would read aloud the book that had the most convincing letter. This was a promise I was ultimately unable to keep, because there was no way to determine which of the incredibly passionate letters was the most persuasive. Here are a few excerpts:

> I think you should read *Bud, Not Buddy* for the next read-aloud because it is a good book for kids. I think we have not read an

African American fiction book. . . . I think the class will go wild like they did with *Holes*. (Dzidzoli)

I love *Bud, Not Buddy*, so I want to compare it to *The Watsons Go to Birmingham*. I want to see if C. P. Curtis wrote the two books alike or different. (Mark)

FIGURE 3.5 Mathias's persuasive letter

> Dear MS. Hahn,
>
>   I think you should read Frindle and then Wringer. I like Frindle because it's about 5th graders and their life. It is also a good story to read over and over again. Actually they both are. Frindle also teaches to experiment with words. Who knows, Someone might get inspiration from the book. It also would be easy to think of a picture for. The same with Wringer. There are lots of events to choose from.
>
> Wringer also is a peaceful book. Well, sort of. It teaches you not to kill. Besides birds were here beafore us. It is a good story about one child who carries on his beliefs to another. Palmer (the frist child) has to fight against his Dad, Mom, and friends, as well as the whole town. Both are good to read and listen to because the stories have a very good feeling.
> Please take this into Consideration.
>
>   sincerely,
>   Mathias Bustamante

FIGURE 3.6 Amanda's persuasive letter

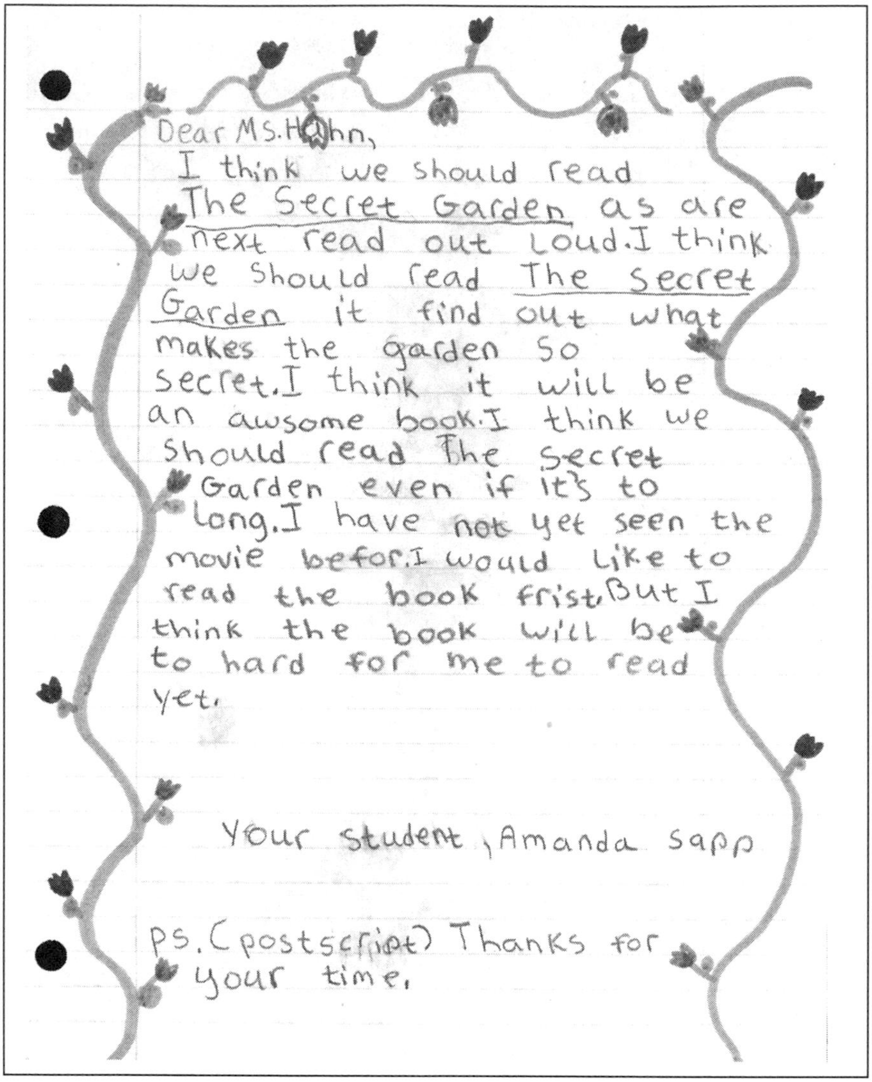

Dear Ms. Hohn,
I think we should read
The Secret Garden as are
next read out Loud. I think
we should read The secret
Garden it find out what
makes the garden so
secret. I think it will be
an awsome book. I think we
should read The secret
Garden even if it's to
long. I have not yet seen the
movie befor. I would Like to
read the book frist, But I
think the book will be
to hard for me to read
yet.

Your student, Amanda Sapp

Ps. (postscript) Thanks for
your time.

I think we should read *The Secret Garden* . . . because we have been reading longer books. Books like *Walk Two Moons* and *Holes*. I know people aren't going to pick the book, because of its size, but isn't it what's inside that counts? I think so. You should never judge a book by its cover or size. At first *Holes* didn't look interesting, but after we got farther into the book I *loved* it. I think that's what people are going to say when they read this book. I also think it's a great book to picture in your mind. I think it would be a great book to stay attached to for a while. (Katie)

I think we should read *Bud, Not Buddy* because it's funny, it's won the Newbery Award, and it's won the Coretta King Award. If it's won two awards it must be good. The Newbery Award is only for books that have the best writing. (Tommy)

Big Topics

Since the conversations we have around our read-alouds allow us to build and develop ideas together, we can determine the size of our "construction site" by the size of the ideas in the read-aloud. Big topics in the read-aloud will result in big conversations that strengthen the community in your classroom. You can talk about peer pressure with *Wringer* (Spinelli); honesty with *Shiloh* (Naylor); race relations with *Maniac Magee* (Spinelli); death with *Fig Pudding* (Fletcher) or *Walk Two Moons* (Creech); European colonialism and the treatment of Native Americans with *Weasel* (DeFelice), *The Sign of the Beaver* (Speare), or *Morning Girl* (Dorris); personal commitment with *Frindle* (Clements).

Two of the biggest topics I have dealt with through read-aloud are race and religion. Our school feels like a Midwestern annex of the United Nations. At last count, more than forty-three nations are or have been represented here. One-third of our 585 students speak another language as their first language at home, and one-sixth of our students are currently in English as a Second Language classes. Every spring we have a huge multicultural celebration, but as a staff we are working to grow beyond the celebration stage—we try to integrate multicultural education into all we do.

Religion

In the spirit of integration, and because I had two Muslim students who I knew would be fasting for Ramadan later in the year, and because my fourth graders were currently or had earlier been in love with Mary Pope Osborne's Magic Tree House series, I chose to read aloud her book *One*

World, Many Religions. As we read, we discussed the similarities and differences in the religions. We referred numerous times to the time line and the map in the back of the book. Some students shared their beliefs, stories about how they had to dress for church, and what their religious classes were like, and some students just listened. We talked about religion-based conflicts in current events, and wondered, based on what we had learned about each religion involved, how religion could be the reason for fighting. When Ramadan came, the class was sensitive to the two students who kept the sunup-to-sundown fast. In mid-December, I drew a continuum on the chalkboard that went from Santa and decorated trees on one end to Christ's birth on the other end. Off the continuum I placed other winter holidays, such as Kwanzaa, winter solstice, Ramadan, and New Year. As we talked about family holiday traditions, we referred to the continuum and saw that each family approaches the winter holiday season in a unique combination of secular, religious, and cultural ways—all equally valid.

Race

Because *One World, Many Religions* had strengthened our sense of community by opening the door for us to talk honestly about religion, I hoped that the right read-alouds would help two of my African American boys in their quest for identity, and would open the door for the whole class to talk honestly about race and discrimination. These two boys were beginning the stage of adolescent racial identity development that Beverly Daniel Tatum describes in *Why Are All the Black Kids Sitting Together in the Cafeteria?* (1997).

> Why do Black youths, in particular, think about themselves in terms of race? Because that is how the rest of the world thinks of them. Our self-perceptions are shaped by the messages that we receive from those around us, and when young Black men and women enter adolescence, the racial content of those messages intensifies. (p. 53–54)

> In adolescence, as race becomes personally salient for Black youth, finding the answer to questions such as, "What does it mean to be a young Black person? How should I act? What

should I do?" is particularly important. And although Black fathers, mothers, aunts and uncles may hold the answers by offering themselves as role models, they hold little appeal for most adolescents. The last thing many fourteen-year-olds [or in the case of my students, precocious eleven-year-olds] want to do is to grow up to be like their parents. It is the peer group, the kids in the cafeteria, who hold the answers to these questions. They know how to be Black. They have absorbed the stereotypical images of Black youth in the popular culture and are reflecting those images in their self-presentation. (p. 60)

Because we all lived in the same classroom, the whole class was, in some sense, going through this stage of racial identity development. One of the boys, Dzidzoli, was an open book, not so much testing the boundaries of acceptability in terms of race and identity as blundering through them. He couldn't understand why some of the girls wouldn't allow him to tell a "blonde joke" during class meeting. He was certain that his joke was not intended to hurt anyone's feelings—it was just funny. It wasn't until I asked him if it would be okay if I told a "black joke"—one that wouldn't hurt anyone's feelings, one that was just funny—that he got quiet and said, "Oh. I get it." He was quick to stereotype whites, but he wouldn't stand for the least stereotyping of blacks. But he also spoke honestly and poignantly about open discrimination that he's felt while trick-or-treating in some neighborhoods, and about the negative, race-based assumptions he can tell people make about him—young black male, therefore must be violent/gang member/dangerous—when he's walking down the street or through the mall.

To begin our conversations of race and discrimination, I read *The Story of Ruby Bridges*, a picture book by Robert Coles, the child psychiatrist who worked with Ruby. I followed that with *Through My Eyes*, Ruby Bridges's autobiography. These books bring race and discrimination to the places that students can relate to best: childhood and school. They allowed us to have conversations (on a ten- and eleven-year-old level) about white guilt for the mistakes of our ancestors, black anger that's based on current discrimination as well as the treatment of their ancestors, positive changes that have taken place in our society since the 1960s, things that haven't changed between blacks and whites since the 1960s, white heroes and black heroes of the civil rights movement, and the kind of world these kids had the power to create—where *human* was the one race that mattered.

I thought we were taking a break from issues of race and discrimination by reading *Holes* next, but we were just warming up. The first time Louis Sachar told us the race of the boys at Camp Green Lake, I stopped reading and we examined what our assumptions had been, based on nicknames, patterns of speech, and who we thought might be in a juvenile detention camp before we had this information about race.

The next read-aloud after *Holes* was *The Watsons Go to Birmingham—1963* by Christopher Paul Curtis. Since I had initiated and validated the class's ongoing discussion of race, it seemed especially important that I read a book by an African American author. More students had expressed an interest in hearing Curtis's *Bud, Not Buddy*, but I chose *The Watsons* instead, because I knew that the time period in which it is set would naturally lead to connections back to Ruby Bridges.

My primary reason for reading *The Watsons* was to continue our discussions of race. But I also chose it because I wanted my students to be as surprised by this book as I was. *The Watsons* had initially entered my classroom library as a freebie from a book club. The cover photographs and the title did not inspire me to put this book on my "to read" pile by my bed; I glued a pocket in it, put in a card for checkout, and added it to my classroom library. After reading *Bud, Not Buddy*, I figured that I had wrongly judged *The Watsons*, so I gave it a try. The hysterical first chapter hooked me and proved how wrong I'd been. When I previewed the book with the students before our first read-aloud, I focused their attention on the photographs and the historical time period, setting them up for a dry and factual piece of historical fiction. I encouraged them to judge this book by its cover. And I could feel their resistance as I began to read. But Byron gets his lips frozen to the rearview mirror of the Watson's car in the first chapter, and any preconceived notions about a dry, factual piece of historical fiction disappeared in the hysterical laughter that this scene evoked.

My students forgave me for deliberately misleading them. In fact, this radical change of mind about *The Watsons* was a more powerful reading lesson than I ever imagined. At the end of the year, when asked, "What else did you learn during read-aloud?," Mark said bluntly, "Don't judge a book by its cover." Katie was a bit more emphatic. "You should *never* judge a book by its cover or title," she said, and Erin's written comment was a bit more eloquent: "I learned that even if a book sounds boring and looks boring then give it a chance it might be good."

Projects

Disciplined spontaneity requires you to be ready for whatever teaching moment comes your way. In *The Watsons*, after Byron's parents punish him for straightening his hair, I stopped and asked my students to talk about the rules for haircuts and hairstyles in their families. In that quick conversation, we touched on how haircuts and -styles can make a statement of personality or rebellion, the importance of hair in some religions, and how hairstyles have changed through history. All our previous conversations about race and religion had prepared me to see the great potential for continuing those conversations around the topic of hair. This time, however, I decided to involve my students' families as well. The next day, I gave this assignment:

> Dear Families,
>
> The book we're reading in read-aloud is *The Watson's Go to Birmingham—1963*. In Chapter 7, Byron, one of the characters, defies his parents by getting "a conk! A process! A do! A butter! A ton of trouble!" We weren't sure what these terms meant until we read on and realized that he had gotten his hair straightened. His father responded by shaving Byron's head.
>
> This started a conversation about haircuts and hairstyles. Most of the students did not believe that parents would have such strict rules about hairstyles as Byron's parents. They were very interested in the social statements that a haircut or -style can make.
>
> It occurred to me that talking about hair could open interesting avenues for learning family stories, and for understanding the role of hair in history and culture.
>
> I would like you (parents and students) to continue our conversation about hair.
>
> ASSIGNMENT: Do an informal investigation on the topic of haircuts and hairstyles. Students, report what you learned on Friday, April 20, 2001.

Investigation technique you MUST use: INTERVIEW
Talk to your parents, AND to someone from a generation earlier than your parents (grandparents, older relatives, older neighbors).

Questions to ask might include the following:

Did your parents/older relatives ever have any rules about hairstyles or haircuts? Do you have any rules in your family?

Did they or anyone they know ever get in trouble because of a hairstyle or haircut?

Are there any rules in your culture about hair? (Culture can mean any or all that apply: white, black, Arabic, Asian, male, female, young, old.)

Do they/you have any strong memories related to hair?

Have they/you ever had (or do you now have) a hairstyle that is intended to make a statement? What statement? Why?

Investigation techniques you COULD use:
Read about hair and hairstyles in books, magazines, encyclopedias, on the Internet, etc., etc.

When you report what you learned, you SHOULD . . .
. . . be ready and willing to talk about what you found out, and have a piece of final draft–quality writing to hand in that tells what you did and what you learned.

Your report COULD include . . .

a poster with your writing on it,

copies of the interview questions you asked and the notes you took on the answers,

copies of the letters you sent and the replies you got back,

photographs,

related information from barbers, hairstylists, and others whose job is hair care,

etc., etc. Be creative.

I intend for this project to be primarily the students' work, but they will need the cooperation of their families. Thank you for sharing your stories and what you know about the role of hair in history and culture. If long-distance phone calls need to be made, I thank you parents in advance for your cooperation. I suggest that the students develop a time line of what they will do and when they will do it so that this project is not done hastily at the last minute. Some of you will be able to do a lot of work on this during spring break; others may not. Don't forget to figure that in when you make your time line. If letters need to be written, students need to do that now so that there is enough time left to get responses.

Any Questions? ASK!"

About a week before the due date, Dzidzoli asked if he could bring in his hair products and show us how he did his hair as a part of his report. I was thrilled that he felt comfortable enough to share this "insider" information with all of us. I extended an invitation to the entire class to bring, on report-sharing day, all the products and tools that they used to fix their hair. I knew my Muslim boy was planning to bring in one of the scarves that his mother wore to keep her head covered, so I approached a third-grade Indian Sikh boy about coming to our class and telling about his turbanlike head covering. He agreed to come with his mother, and in talking to her about his *Patka*, I learned that it is not simply a head covering. Under it is the most important symbol of the Sikh religion: uncut hair, which is regarded as an indication of living in harmony with the will of God. The power of using hair as the starting point for discussions about culture, race, and religion was beginning to become clear to me.

The day the hair reports were due evolved into a daylong celebration of culture and religion, similarities and differences. We began with Mrs. Neki and Preet teaching us the five symbols of Sikhism. Mrs. Neki masterfully extended the idea of deliberately looking different as a way to set oneself apart for reasons of religion to the general idea that each person should be proud of his or her own differences, and respect the differences of others. The tone for the day was set.

Next we shared hair products and tools. Dzidzoli greased and brushed his hair, and as the students passed around the products and tools, we created a time line on the chalkboard to compare how often we each washed our hair. We had a continuum that spanned from daily for Caucasian hair to monthly for African American hair that was braided. We marveled that some products were necessary for removing oil from hair, whereas others were specifically for adding oil to hair.

FIGURE 3.7 Mark's hair project

Mark

Everybody in the world at one time had hair. In the 1700's American men started to wear long, powdery, white wigs; Like George Washington, but Thomas Jefferson only wore his own red hair. There are many kinds of hairdos, like ponytails, buzzes, and much, much more. A long time ago in Egypt they had to shave their head bald. They wore wigs made out of human hair, straw, leaves, and wool. They also had a style where they wore beards; even women wore beards! Back in the 1600 and 1700's men usually wore much longer wigs than women. They also thought men should wear ponytails and not women. Back then women used dolls to show people the styles. They would sew clothes for the dolls that were in style. Then they'd fix the doll's hair so it would look like the hairdo that was in style. In the 1960's men wore long hair and afros. Women wore long, flowing hair; those were the fads then. One time my Uncle wore bangs to school and got sent to the principal's office because their principal didn't allow boys to wear bangs at his school. In the 1970's and 1980's bleaching your hair was the fad. In the 1990's dred locks, page boy "Princess Diana look", and baldness were the fads. There are even more fads throughout the years.

FIGURE 3.7 *continued*

> Rules from parents....................
> short hair only
> No dying hair yet
>
> Getting in trouble with hair........
> Once my Uncle got his hair cut, but
> left it too long and his parents made
> him go back and get it cut shorter.
> My neighbor, Mrs. Amin, and her sister
> cut their bangs off.
> My neighbor, Mrs. Johnson, went to
> middle school and had to cut off her
> bangs, because they were too long.
>
> Made fun of.........
> My Aunt used "Sun In" to lighten
> her hair.
> My Dad hears comments about going
> bald by my brother and me.
>
> There are many kinds of hair
> styles in the world. I think
> people's culture makes the biggest
> difference in their hairstyle.

When we finally got to the sharing of the reports, the students had a wide variety of final products—posters, written reports, scrapbooks—and an incredible collection of family stories about hair. Some also interviewed neighbors or family friends who gave them insight into cultures other than their own. Still others focused on the history of hairstyles from prehistoric to modern times.

What happened with *The Watsons Go to Birmingham—1963* in one classroom with one particular group of children is an example of how the read-aloud can reflect the existing classroom community, contribute toward building and strengthening the classroom community, and even extend the classroom community to the local community and society at large.

General Strategies

S ome reading strategies are used when reading aloud (or reading) either fiction or nonfiction. In the classroom vignettes that follow, a few of the more important general reading strategies that are taught during read-aloud are described.

Previewing a book thoroughly before reading and activating prior knowledge get the listener or reader ready for better comprehension. Reading with expression either orally or silently forces the listener or the reader to be attentive to the myriad of clues the author gives the reader about how the story should "sound." Visualizing the text is another way each person responds to the author's writing. Every reader or listener needs to have strategies in place for remembering where she left off and for figuring out vocabulary in context. Read-aloud discussions of all genres are filled with teaching and learning when the teacher works to lift the level of the talk, and when she acknowledges all the responses of her students.

Previewing Strategies

At the beginning of every new read-aloud, you have the opportunity to model book selection and previewing strategies.

When we were getting ready to start *Weasel* (DeFelice), our discussion went like this:

"If you were in the library and this title caught your eye, and you took this book off the shelf, what's the next thing you would do to see if you wanted to check it out and read it?" I asked.

"I'd look at the cover," someone answered. So we studied the cover. I took the book around the room and let every table of students have a good long look and tell what they were noticing: a kid, a club, a swamp, a man with a gun, it's night, there are birds, they are wearing old-time clothes.

"What would you do next?" I asked. Shane said he would look inside the cover or on the back and read the blurb. So I did.

"Now what?" I continued. Ethan said he would read the first page. Tyler added that he likes to read the last page, too. (I disagreed with Tyler on a personal note—I *never* read the ending first—but I told him I know many people do. I even know two best friends who almost come to blows over this in bookstores when they are shopping for books together. One is a "never read the ending first" person, and the other is an "always read the last page first" person. Somehow they have managed to remain friends.)

The whole first chapter of *Weasel* is not much more than a page long. In it, a silent stranger comes to the door of the cabin of two children who are awaiting their father's return from a hunting trip. The stranger is carrying the children's mother's locket. When I had finished the chapter, I asked Ethan, "If this had been a book you were trying to decide whether to read, and you had read just that first page, would you read on?" Of course he would! Who could resist the hook that Cynthia DeFelice, the author, had dangled before us?

Prior Knowledge

We were reading *Christmas in Camelot* by Mary Pope Osborne. It was the week after winter break, but the opportunity to read the newest book in a familiar series was too good to pass up. All but about two of my students had read a Magic Tree House book before this one.

The need to activate prior knowledge is often linked to some aspect of the story—understanding a certain kind of character, the place as well as the time period of the setting, or the topic of the story. Before we read on the first day, we had talked a little about Camelot, King Arthur, and the Knights of the Round Table. The avid readers of the series knew that Jack and Annie had performed some tasks for Morgan Le Fay, the librarian in Camelot.

The prior knowledge to activate for this book also included that of book structure—it has a prologue. We talked about what a prologue is ("like an introduction," Youngghil explained) and how it functions. In this case, it gives the reader of a series book some basic information about what has happened in the previous books.

But it was on the second day before reading that my generic question, "Does anyone want to say anything before I start reading?" resulted in full-blown activation of prior knowledge. I even used those words to describe to the students what they were doing.

After my question, there were the usual negative mumblings from those who just wanted to get right to the book. But Shane had his hand up, so there would be some talk before reading on this day. He made a connection between the book and a cartoon show on TV that is a take-off on the Camelot story, with children as the knights. Other students had seen TV shows and movies that were directly or indirectly related to the Arthurian legend. Once Shane got them started, the connections were building and building, like the strands of a spider's web, from student to student. Then we were more ready than ever to read. Before I started, I said, "What we were just doing was a really important and really smart thing that readers do before they read a book or before they read the next chapter in their book. Good readers think of all the connections they can make to the book. That's called activating your prior knowledge. It's like building a web inside your brain of everything you already know and all the connections you can make to the book. When you activate your prior knowledge, you give the new information in the book a place to plug in. Human brains can learn new information only when there is a place to plug it in. If you can't plug it in to what you already know, it just sort of slides out of your brain." Not very scientific, but I hoped it was graphic enough so that my students would not view the time spent getting ready to read as wasted.

Reading with Expression

It just about goes without saying that when you are reading aloud to your students, you should read with theatrical expression, dramatic timing, and authentic enthusiasm. Mem Fox says, "There's no exact right way of reading aloud, other than to try to be as expressive as possible. As we read a story, we need to be aware of our body position, our eyes and their expression, or eye contact with the child or children, our vocal variety, and our general facial animation. But each of us will have our own special way of doing it" (2001, p. 40).

When Joyce Zawaly, a fourth-grade teacher, has reading conferences with her students, she listens to her students read a passage from their independent reading book that they have selected and practiced. If their reading is monotone and word-by-word, she coaches them to be more expressive, reminding them of the way she models expressive reading during read-aloud. Joyce even goes so far as to create a different voice for almost every character in the books she reads aloud. She then includes in the child's learning plan for reading a goal about reading aloud with more expression, and she sends the child off with instructions to practice for a week or two and then report back to her.

This is an appropriate reading goal. If children read more expressively aloud, chances are it will carry over into their silent reading. Just as comprehension is enhanced by a reader's ability to visualize or "see" the story, it is enhanced by a reader's ability to accurately "hear" the story: the sounds in the story, and the voices of different characters, along with the tone (angry, joking, excited, etc.) and pitch (hollering, whispering, etc.) of their voices.

Visualization

After word solving, visualization is the most critical comprehension strategy. Visualizing what the words in a text mean or describe is the essence of reading. Everything we can do to model for students how and what we visualize, and every opportunity we can give them to further develop their ability to visualize, will help to develop stronger readers.

Throughout read-aloud, the teacher can stop to interject her visualization, or "mind picture," or ask students to describe what they are seeing at a certain point. I sometimes call this the movie that plays in my mind while I read. As if there is a movie screen inside my brain, I can "see" what's going on in the story.

Even after you have finished the book, it is powerful to share how you visualized the characters, the setting, or certain scenes in the story. During a student-parent book club, I asked each person to share how they had visualized the edifice in Lois Lowry's *Gathering Blue*. Every reader's understanding of the story was deepened by hearing that someone pictured the building like a church, someone else like a government building, another person only from the inside and never the outside, and someone always from an elevated point of view. It was amazing to realize that we had all read the same words but had all "seen" a different book inside our minds.

When I began the ritual at the end of our main read-alouds of having one student create a big picture of a favorite part of the book for our gallery of read-alouds while the others created a small picture of a favorite part for a class book, I never imagined how complex, multilayered, and revealing it would be. The pictures my fourth graders created at the beginning of the school year were unimaginative and lacking details from the story. Suddenly, a little more than halfway through the school year, their pictures began to be filled with detail. They accepted it when I refused to let them look at the pictures in or on the cover of the books and said, "Why not just draw what you see in your mind? That's all an illustration is—someone else's visualization of the author's words."

I wish I knew where this leap of creativity and ability to visualize the story came from. Was it that particular book, the time of year, the number of books we'd read during read-aloud, the general maturity of the class, or some other factor? There are too many variables to know.

Strategies for Remembering Where You Left Off

One of the strategies good readers use before starting to read again is remembering what was happening in the story when they left off. This important strategy can be taught during read-aloud in a variety of ways.

Get a Running Start—Modeling a Strategy for Remembering

At the beginning of read-aloud, don't just pick up right where you left off the day before. Get a running start on the new material by reading a few paragraphs from where you left off. Tell your students why you are doing that. Talk about how rereading helps the reader remember what was happening and how that will help today's reading make more sense.

What Happened Yesterday in Read-Aloud?—Sharing Responsibility for Remembering

You can simply start your read-aloud by asking a question such as, "What was happening yesterday when we left off?" However, if you frequently start your read-aloud like that, you might discover that the same student or students answer every time. They are good at remembering where you left off—perhaps even better than you are sometimes! But because they are so good at remembering where you were in the story the day before, they are the ones who least need practice in this strategy. You can use several other strategies to get more than one student involved in the process of remembering what was happening when you left off, and to support the students who still need to learn or practice how to hold the story in their mind so that they can retrieve it the next day.

Say One Word—Sharing Responsibility for Remembering

Ask for volunteers who will "say one word, and only one word, about what was going on the last time we read." This gives your eager and able child a chance to participate, but it also rewards creative thinking and allows everyone in the class a chance to collaboratively reconstruct the story one word at a time.

We were near the middle of *Meet Addy* (Porter) when I began read-aloud time by asking my students to "say one word, and only one word, about what was going on the last time we read."

John started things off with "Planning." Addy and her mother were planning to run away from slavery to freedom. That was just enough to jog many students' minds. Lots of hands popped up. The next student said, "Run away." Another very obvious, very literal choice. Amanda was creative. She said, "Sadness." She went beyond the literal to the inferential. Shane said, "Leave." Tori added, "Underground Railroad," apologizing for using two words, but explaining that they had to go together. Then Preet reminded us of another layer in the story with "Esther," the baby sister Addy must leave behind. That led Youngghil to say, "Poppa," and John to say, "Sam," the other family members Addy must leave behind. From somewhere in the room came the word "Freedom." I thought that summary was good enough for me to begin read-aloud for the day.

Talk to Your Neighbor—Guiding Students Toward Independence in Remembering

When you use the Get a Running Start Strategy, you are modeling a way to remember where you left off in a story. In the modeling phase of the Apprenticeship Model, the teacher does all the work. When you use What Happened Yesterday, or Say One Word, the whole class takes part in a shared experience of remembering where you left off. In the shared phase of the Apprenticeship Model, the teacher offers lots of support as the whole class works together to make meaning. When you say to your students, "Turn to your neighbor and talk about what was happening when we left off yesterday," you are guiding them toward independence. In the guided phase of the Apprenticeship Model, the learner is still supported, but the teacher plays a smaller role.

When you bring each of these ways of remembering into your reading workshop, your students will learn to independently, habitually, and mindfully use the important strategy of remembering where they left off before reading on. Then, in individual conferences with your students, you can assess your teaching and their learning by making it a point to ask which way of remembering they have found the most helpful and are using regularly.

Sequencing, Summarizing, and Retelling

Sequencing, summarizing, and retelling can be used as ways to practice the strategy of remembering, but they are also outcomes on their own. Sequencing is a foundational skill, upon which summarizing and retelling are built. A summary tells in one or two sentences what a story or chapter is about. A retelling is a more detailed description of what a story or chapter is about. Before students are asked to independently sequence, summarize, or retell, it is wise to model, share, and guide the practice of each during read-aloud.

Remember to teach lightly during read-aloud. Too much teaching—for example, sequencing, retelling, or summarizing every chapter of a read-aloud book—can destroy the students' enthusiasm for and enjoyment of read-aloud time. It will become another work time driven by the teacher's agenda, rather than a time of enjoyment and natural learning. If you apply the Apprenticeship Model, you need to plan for only two or three times during the book when you step away from the story to do some paper-and-pencil kind of work—during the shared and guided phases, and perhaps during the independent phase. You might have students independently apply what they've learned about sequencing, summarizing, or retelling to the book they are reading independently during reading workshop.

Although much of what you teach during read-aloud is best taught spontaneously, driven by the book, your knowledge as a reader, or your students' questions and comments, there is a place in read-aloud for planned teaching. If skills such as sequencing, summarizing, and retelling are taught early in the year, students will be able to use them, refine them, and build on them all year long. Your first read-alouds will probably be shorter books, so that you can help your class build the stamina for longer stories. That means that in three short read-alouds at the beginning of the year, you can lay important groundwork not only for listening and remembering the read-aloud, but for sequencing, retelling, and summarizing independently.

Instead of saying, "What happened yesterday when we read?" you can model the sequencing you will be asking the students to do by saying, "You know that it is important for readers to be able to remember the events of a chapter or book so that when they read on, it keeps making sense. It is also important to remember the events in order. Let me show you an easy way to put the events in order by using sticky notes." Write one event per sticky note, and deliberately write them in a random order so that you can model how you would move the notes to create the correct sequence. Later in the book, you can have the students tell the events that you will write on the sticky notes, and then you can share the work of putting them in order. Still later, students can work in partners or groups to write events on sticky notes and order them in a guided experience. They can practice the skill of sequencing in their independent reading or using another section of the read-aloud.

After you have worked on sequencing, perhaps in your next read-aloud book, you might say, "Sometimes when a reader wants to remember what happened in a chapter they've read or a book they've read, they write a summary, [or retelling]. Let me show you how I would summarize [or retell] what happened in yesterday's reading." Use sticky notes to get the events in proper sequence, then use them to write the summary [or retelling]. Later in the book, you can say, "Let's work together on a summary [or retelling] of yesterday's chapter." With you writing the sticky notes and helping the class to organize their thoughts and create a concise statement [summary] or detailed description [retelling], it will be a shared experience. Still later, when you have all worked together on a summary or retelling, you can have students at a table or with partners brainstorm the events in the most recent section or chapter of the book, each writing one event on a sticky note, then ordering the sticky notes and together, in a guided experience, writing a summary or retelling from their notes.

Vocabulary in Context

In my classroom, it's okay to ask what a word means. Sometimes it is even necessary for survival, because I make it a point to talk over my students' heads as much as possible. How else will they learn new vocabulary? "Make sure you have ample reading material," I say, and so they'll know what to do, someone asks, "What's 'ample'?" I also insist on precise use of words. Even if I know perfectly well what they're talking about, I won't have a conversation about "things" or "stuff." "'Things? Stuff'? What exactly are you talking about?" I ask, and then I help the child name or define his or her topic. During read-aloud, I stop occasionally to define or highlight unusual or difficult words in the text. All of this focus on vocabulary and language has set the tone in my classroom for a natural curiosity about words.

When I read *Weasel*, our third long book of the year, I knew I must have paused enough times to ask, "Do you know what _____ means?" or "What's a _____?" or "Show me how you'd look if you were _____." I knew because students started asking for the meanings of words or phrases while I read. Yes, they interrupted me while I was reading, but they did it the way I interrupt myself: quietly and discreetly.

I was reading, "I watched Weasel take another big drink out of the jug, and it gave me an idea. No man could drink as much as Weasel had been drinking without having to answer a call of nature," when a quiet voice asked, "What's a 'call of nature'?" My answer modeled the use of context clues. "Well, he's had a lot to drink . . ." Giggles told me they understood.

I read on: "So far I hadn't said a word, so as not to take a chance on making Weasel mad, but now I blurted, 'I need to go out.'

"Weasel stared at me dumbly.

"'To the privy,' I explained."

"What's a 'privy'?" someone asked. I gave the question back to the class: "Anyone know?"

"An outhouse." "An outdoor bathroom." "Like at camp or a state park." "Eeewww!" I read on.

Later in the book, during the part when Nathan's father explains the government's Indian removal policy, I read, "They didn't put much value on the life of a Shawnee.

"I thought of the we-gi-wa, and Ezra's wife."

"What's a 'we-gi-wa'?" someone asked.

"It's his house, remember?" came the answer from across the room. I read on.

Vocabulary Hounds

It seems that every year, one or two students will emerge as unpaid anonymous assistant teachers during read-aloud. One year it was Katie, who led the way in responding eloquently to books in our discussions, and who was unashamed to cry openly when Brad died in *Fig Pudding* (Fletcher) and when Gram died in *Walk Two Moons* (Creech). Her enthusiastic, honest, insightful responses led the whole class to deeper understanding of books. Read-aloud wouldn't have been the same without her.

Another year, I had two assistants who helped me to focus the class on vocabulary. I am the Head Vocabulary Hound during read-alouds, always on the lookout for words the students might need to know to make sense of the story. Preet distinguished himself as Assistant Vocabulary Hound in the first few days of school. As I read aloud *The Secret Knowledge of Grown-ups* (Wisniewski), I was introduced to Preet's natural curiosity about words. In the book, the leader of the thumb gang wears a T-shirt that says, "I'm opposable." Gales of laughter rang out, but I wasn't sure if it was because they really understood the double meaning of opposable, or because it's just funny to see a big, tough thumb in a T-shirt. Later, when packing up to go home, Preet was still thinking about the vocabulary in the book when he asked, "What's 'opposable'?" That was just the start. Preet continued to keep me and the class focused on interesting and unusual vocabulary throughout the year, and he went on to become close friends with the thesaurus, agonizing over word choice in his own writing.

Tyler got his start as my other Assistant Vocabulary Hound as we read *Because of Winn-Dixie* by Kate DiCamillo. On the day I started the read-aloud, I modeled the way I preview a book by examining the cover before I begin reading. I pointed out a word in the title that might make anyone who lived in the South curious about this book. Winn-Dixie is a grocery store chain in the South, I explained. Readers there might be thinking, "Because of the grocery store? What's this book going to be about?"

At the end of the first chapter, Tyler's hand shot up. "Isn't a preacher like a priest?" he asked. I answered his question, confirming that we call the leader of worship in a Catholic church a priest, but the leader of worship in other Christian churches a preacher. But that's not all Tyler was thinking about. "So how can the Preacher have a wife and a kid?" he followed up, revealing that there had been another layer to his question. This exchange served as a reminder that a reader's knowledge or understanding of the vocabulary can alter his understanding of the story.

At the end of Chapter 5, Tyler's hand shot up again. Impeccable timing! Patience mixed with persistence—a rare combination in a nine-year-old. This time he wanted to know, "What's a 'picket quick'?"

"Pick-It-Quick," I clarified, exaggerating the pauses between the words. By the look on his face, I could tell I had failed. This is a phrase a reader needs to see to understand, so I wrote it on the board and said, "Let's go back to the story and see what we know about what it is, and put that together with the name to decide for ourselves." We decided it was some kind of convenience store, and I read on.

We had several other interesting vocabulary encounters as I read aloud *Because of Winn-Dixie*. In Chapter 5, Winn-Dixie (a dog named after a grocery store) is allowed to come to church with India Opal and her father, the Preacher, but must remain outside, tied to a tree. When the Preacher begins preaching, Winn-Dixie begins howling. The students were amused by my howling, but I wanted them to know that I was reading "words" from the book. Plus, I was having a hard time "pronouncing" one of them. I wrote on the chalkboard the three howl words that Winn-Dixie howls: Aaaaaarrooo, Arrroooowwww, and Arruiiiiipppp. Together we worked out what each would sound like, and I reread the passage where Winn-Dixie howls, with my students playing the part of Winn-Dixie. I imagine that caused a moment of puzzlement in the two classrooms adjacent to ours.

When India Opal is listening to Miss Franny tell the story of the bear that came into the library and learns that he left with the copy of *War and Peace* Miss Franny threw at him, India Opal says, "Nuh-uh," and I heard an echo in the classroom as one or more students made that familiar noise that means "no" or "no way" in child-speak. "That's just what the author wrote," I said. "Look, here's how she spelled it." I wrote it on the board beside the howl words and Pick-It-Quick. "This author uses a lot of funny words," someone noted.

"I think she just writes the way people really talk," I countered. I decided not to directly teach about dialect at this time, but made a mental note that I might want to read aloud *Shiloh* (Naylor), both for more explicit examples of dialect and for the great dog story comparisons we could make to *Because of Winn-Dixie*.

Before I started reading *Because of Winn-Dixie*, I told my students that the reason I picked it was that I had fallen in love with the dog in this story, and I wanted to see if they would, too. That was the honest truth. I had no idea when I chose this book what vocabulary I might teach (including dog "words"), and I had no way of knowing what vocabulary would pique the interest of or confuse the students. The joy of read-aloud is following where the book and where the students lead.

Better Talk

There was nothing unusual about the way read-aloud started (*Meet Addy* by Connie Porter). I asked, "Any questions or comments before we get started on Chapter 2?" Someone commented that they liked the book. Someone wondered how old Addy's brother Sam was. Someone else wondered who would take care of Addy's baby sister Esther when everybody went to work during the day.

Then I called on Michelle. "I have a question," she began. "What does it mean when it says that Addy's parents could only cry on the inside when they saw Sam whipped?"

Sometimes read-aloud discussions resemble what fourth-grade teacher Joyce Zawaly terms "ping-pong" connections with question followed by answer followed by comment followed by unrelated comment. But Michelle's was the kind of question I knew we could stay with for more than just an answer. It was the kind of question that would allow us to develop theories, more like an archaeological dig than a ping-pong match.

I asked if anyone had an idea to answer Michelle's question. I called on someone who thought the reason had most to do with adults being able to control their emotions better than children. The next person I called on commented on a different topic, but I said, "Hold all your other thoughts until we are finished working on this one. Does anyone have any other possible ideas?" Next we explored the idea that it had more to do with being a slave than being an adult. Perhaps Addy's parents weren't allowed to cry in public. We took a vote. The class was split between whether it was more about being an adult or more about being a slave. I decided to stretch their thinking with a theory of my own. "Tell me what you think of this. It just occurred to me and I don't think it's any more right than your ideas. Remember when we read the history from the back of the book and it said that slave owners sometimes split up families? I'm thinking that if Addy's parents showed how much they loved Sam by crying when they saw him whipped, they would be giving the owner information that he could use to hurt them. If he knew how much they cared, he might be more likely to split up their family."

Toward the end of the book, Addy stumbles into a Confederate camp. Luckily, she is mistaken for the camp water boy. As she gets a drink of water for one of the soldiers, "Addy lowered her head, touched the cowrie shell briefly, and began to move. Inside she was shaking, but on the outside she was walking straight and strong past the sleeping soldiers. She picked up the bucket and brought it to the soldier." I looked over at Michelle and could see by the excited look on her face that she was thinking exactly what I was thinking. "Michelle! What's going on here?" I asked.

She practically bounced out of her chair. "It's like at the beginning, except now she is learning to keep her feelings inside to protect herself!" she answered proudly.

Promoting better talk in read-aloud discussions requires the teacher to be alert when students make comments that go deeper than the surface of the story. Better talk means teaching students how to build an idea together through conversation rather than simply sharing unrelated thoughts. (See Chapter 12, "A Curriculum of Talk" in Lucy Calkins's *The Art of Teaching Reading*.) Better talk occurs when the teacher prepares for it with her own reading. Because fifth-grade teacher Julia Barthelmes has read all of Sharon Creech's books, she can help her students take their comparisons of Creech's books beyond the obvious surface elements and into the deeper theme of journeys—physical journeys and journeys of personal growth. "Whether or not their little fifth-grade minds can really wrap their heads around that a whole lot, at least they start thinking that there's more there than just the 'top story.' They're just starting to think about that," she said.

Amazing Response to Simple Text

I chose *Christmas in Camelot* by Mary Pope Osborne with the criteria "newest book in a beloved series," and "quick read after winter break." It was not chosen with any thought that it would prompt the children to do some of their best thinking during read-aloud so far. But perhaps it wouldn't have mattered what I had chosen next. Perhaps their growth as listeners and thinkers during read-aloud simply progresses from book to book, regardless of what the book is; they do better thinking with more practice. Based on the kind of mind work my students did with this book, however, there is a case to be made that simple (but of course well-written) read-alouds can inspire the best thinking.

Sometimes there is no need for you to say, "Turn to your neighbor and talk." Sometimes you just have to step back and let them take over.

This happened in *Christmas in Camelot* when Jack and Annie got to the circle of dancers and Annie discovered that the three knights King Arthur had sent on the quest for the Water of Memory and Imagination were also dancing in the circle. "I get it!" shouted Nicole, and the room erupted into excited conversations in which students predicted, inferred, connected, and summarized. A small group that was following along in their own copy of the book studied the double-spread illustration of the circle of dancers until they found three tiny figures who must have been the knights because they didn't have wings. The conversations continued for one or two minutes, and I knew they were ready for me to read again when I heard, "Read on!" I did.

When Jack and Annie made it through the gates to the Otherworld and they heard music, someone quietly commented, "It's the music and joy that was robbed from Camelot." What an inference! Wow.

Youngghil had checked out a simple Gail Gibbons book about King Arthur and the Knights of the Round Table when the class had library time. He had the book open as I was reading. When Jack and Annie receive the cup from Sir Galahad, he pointed to one of the pictures and said, "The cup!" In Gibbons's book, the cup was actually the Holy Grail. I started to say, "That's a different cup. It was the object of many quests in the story of Camelot. It's called the—" when Tyler chimed in, "The Holy Grail! It was the cup that caught the blood of Christ when he was crucified." We compared what Tyler knew with the information in the Gibbons book that said the Holy Grail was the cup used by Christ at the Last Supper.

"So King Arthur was a Christian?" Tsilat wondered.

In this one little interchange, a two- or three-minute interruption of the read-aloud, we had compared text with text, compared two texts with prior knowledge, and drawn a conclusion based on the evidence. Wow again.

John is looking at the illustration that shows Jack and Annie fighting a dragon with flaming torches. He laughs skeptically, "Look at that! Fighting a fire-breathing dragon with those little fire sticks!"

I glance at the picture and say, "But it's not a fire-breathing dragon." The picture doesn't show it, but John knows just where to look in the text to read me the part that says, "The creature hissed and blue flame shot from its mouth." John has a good point, and I take a breath to agree with him. But it occurs to me that later in the story when we find out how Jack and Annie actually defeat the dragon after taking sips of the Water of Memory and Imagination, we will need to come back to this illustration and think about exactly how Osborne gave her characters the ability to defeat the fire-breathing dragon with little fire sticks. So instead of agreeing with John, I tell him to hold his thought about the illustration and that we'll talk about it after the dragon is defeated.

It's stunning how perceptive they are, how smart their thinking is, how discoveries and comments and background knowledge from individuals come together to make a collective response that none of them could have managed on their own. How the parts make an amazing whole. But it's like building a jigsaw puzzle without knowing ahead of time what any of the pieces look like or who holds the pieces. Nevertheless, a beautiful picture or pattern emerges as you read and discuss.

 5

Fiction Strategies

The strategies highlighted in the classroom vignettes in this chapter are a sampling of the reading strategies for fiction that one might teach during read-aloud. Rather than providing an exhaustive list of every possible fiction strategy, I have chosen examples that highlight different kinds of teaching one can do during read-aloud: spontaneous teaching prompted by student comments (Analyze the Plot, In Case You Didn't Already Notice, and The Author Is Winking), planned teaching (Questioning, Text-to-Text Connections, Historical Facts, Trust the Author, and Read-Aloud Props), and inquiry-based teaching that results from a reflective stance taken by the teacher (Rereading).

Analyze the Plot

We had come to the end of Chapter 12 in *Weasel* (DeFelice). Nathan, Molly, and their father are coming home from Ezra's we-gi-wa. Molly has helped their father recover from having his leg caught in one of Weasel's traps, and Nathan has confronted, been kidnapped by, and escaped from Weasel. "That feels like the end," Preet said.

When a child hands you a great lesson, never refuse the gift.

I stopped reading and we analyzed the plot. I didn't tell them that's what we were doing, but as we discussed all the things that made it feel like an ending and why an author would put an "ending" in the middle of a book, we were certainly analyzing the plot.

Because we were at a transition point in the text, it was also a perfect time to make predictions about the second half of the book. Preet predicted that Nathan would get revenge, or that Weasel would come and attack the family now that they were home. Jessica and Kyle also thought Weasel would come back, but someone else thought Nathan would run away and kill Weasel. Michelle offered that at the very end, Weasel might say was sorry for all he had done. Although I accepted all the other predictions with no more than a nod, we stopped and talked about Michelle's. In many stories, the bad character undergoes a transformation at the end (think of the Grinch), and Michelle was using her knowledge of story structure to make her prediction. However, predictions must also be based on information in the text at hand. When I asked Michelle what evidence we had in the story so far that Weasel might change his ways, she was stumped, and she began to understand how to base her predictions first and foremost on the evidence in the text.

In Case You Didn't Already Notice

Sometimes authors give the reader information that they withhold from the characters in the story, and then the reader feels smart, smarter than the character who cannot see what is perfectly clear to the reader. Other times authors make it easy for the reader to make predictions and then confirm them with evidence in the text. Often the author offers the reader several chances to make an obvious prediction until finally, it is as if—bonk!—the author has hit the reader over the head with the information, as if to say, "Reader, if you haven't already figured this out, I am going to tell you what is happening." A perfect example of this is in *Holes*. Long after my students had figured out that Stanley Yelnats is a palindrome, Louis Sachar includes this information in the story, just in case the readers hadn't figured it out by themselves.

At the end of *Weasel*, Ezra leaves this note for Molly in the stone fence when he leaves for Kansas to find his Shawnee wife's relatives:

Dear Molly,
    Your letter was true. I am gon to Kansis to find her kin. Tell Nathan be happy in the hat. Weezl is small now. I remmber you allwaze.
    Your frend, Ezra

After I read Ezra's note, someone asked, "What does it mean, 'Weasel is small now'?" We had a long discussion, and several students shared insightful thoughts about both Nathan's and Ezra's personal growth in coming to grips with the effect of Weasel in their lives, and in doing away with the need for revenge.

A page later, almost as if on cue, Molly asked, "What does he mean, though, 'Weasel is small now'?" Nathan's explanation in the book barely touched on the depth of my students' thoughts, but it left them with the sense that they had the power to understand the story beyond even what the author might include.

We felt the author hitting us over the head with information after we had already figured something out several times in *Meet Addy* (Porter). At one point, Addy has just served dinner to Master Stevens and a guest. She is standing quietly in the corner with her face gone blank and empty. She hears,

"I got them all trained good," said Master Stevens. "That's why it's such a shame to let any of them go."

The gasps from my students told me they were making an accurate prediction that "them" might be some of Addy's family members.

Addy's stomach turned when she heard Master Stevens say those words. *Let any of them go?* she thought. *What he mean, let go?*

Here, if the reader has picked up on the hint in what Master Stevens said that some of Addy's family members may be at risk of being sold, the reader can feel smarter than the character in the book. If it has not occurred to the reader that he or she should be thinking about Addy's family, this is another, more obvious hint:

"This boy you got for me," [more gasps—Sam, Addy's brother!] said the man, "how can I be sure he won't run on me, too? I know he's run before." [gasp! Sam for sure!]

Again the author gives us more clues, and then adds a little extra twist about Poppa that the students didn't see coming:

"I taught him a lesson with the whip last time he ran off," Master Stevens answered, "and you'll have his father, too. [gasp!] His father can control him."

They were talking about selling Sam and Poppa! Addy just knew they were.

Bonk! In case the reader wasn't paying attention to the clues, the author finally "hits the reader over the head" with the information.

Holes is filled with clues and explanations for the alert reader or listener: the jars of peaches that become the "sploosh," the onions that protect Stanley and Zero from the yellow-spotted lizards, and the revelation of why Zero knew so much about Stanley's "crime." Best of all, in the last chapter, Louis Sachar writes, "The reader might find it interesting, however, that Stanley's father invented his cure for foot odor the day after the great-great-grandson of Elya Yelnats carried the great-great-great-grandson of Madame Zeroni up the mountain."

Some of my students hadn't made that connection in the course of the story. The first time I read *Holes*, I didn't either. Somehow I had never connected Hector "Zero" Zeroni's last name to Madame Zeroni. I remember how pleasantly surprised I was when Sachar made sure I realized that all the story lines in the book had suddenly come together. Each subsequent time I have read *Holes*, I have found more and more clues that Sachar planted throughout the book, and my admiration for his writing grows with each reading. To give my students a hint of all they might have missed on the first reading, I took them back, after we finished the book, to Chapter 7, page 38, and read:

> He remembered Madame Zeroni telling him that she had a son in America. Elya was forever looking for him. He'd walk up to a complete stranger and ask if they knew someone named Zeroni, or had ever heard of anyone named Zeroni.
>
> No one did. Elya wasn't sure what he'd do if he ever found Madame Zeroni's son anyway. Carry him up a mountain and sing the pig lullaby to him?

They were stunned to realize that on page 38, Sachar had revealed the conclusion of the book.

The Author Is Winking

I was reading from *Christmas in Camelot* on the day author Mary Pope Osborne and I made the students' chins drop in unison. We were at the part where Jack and Annie are considering how the gifts they've been given might help them.

> "The first gift is the Christmas Knight's cloak," said Annie.
> "Yeah, I guess it's supposed to help us somehow," said Jack.
> He unbuttoned the cloak from around his neck. Then he held it out to get a good look at it.
> "Maybe it can make us invisible," said Annie.

"Like in Harry Potter!" Becca interjected excitedly.

"Wait! Listen to this—I think Mary Pope Osborne is winking at the reader," I answered.

> "Maybe it can make us invisible," said Annie.
> "That's nuts," said Jack.
> "Seriously," she said, "cloaks sometimes do that in stories."

Every chin in the room dropped. The students had perhaps their first experience of looking over the heads of the characters in the book and seeing the author in their mind's eye, looking directly at them, the readers, and winking. They winked back.

Questioning

The strategy of asking questions before, during, and after reading is important for the comprehension of both fiction and nonfiction. "When our students ask questions and search for answers, we know that they are monitoring comprehension and interacting with the text to construct meaning, which is exactly what we hope for in developing readers" (Harvey and Goudvis 2000).

With one of her early read-alouds, fourth-grade teacher Joyce Zawaly models the questioning strategy. She guides her students from indiscriminate questions-for-the-sake-of-questions to thoughtfully crafted questions that require higher levels of thinking. The structure of fiction naturally supports this shift from many surface questions to fewer deeper questions. In the beginning of a fiction book, the author gives the reader basic information about the characters, the setting, and the plot. Often the author deliberately causes the reader to wonder and question as a device to hook the reader, so that he or she will want to read on and find out what happens, who the mysterious character is, or in exactly what time and place the story is set. As the story progresses, the readers' early questions are answered and larger, deeper, more complicated questions are possible because the reader understands the basic story line.

This year Joyce was ready to begin reading *Shiloh* (Naylor) when she decided it was time to teach questioning. She chose *Shiloh* because she knew it would afford the opportunity to explore thoughtful questions, and because she loves the story.

At the end of every chapter in *Shiloh*, Joyce charted all of her students' questions. As they read on, they coded their questions with an A for a question answered, a BK for a question that was answered with background knowledge, an N for a question not answered, and an R for a question that required research. After the first few chapters, their list was very long—too long. To help the students learn to refine their questions, Joyce asked, "Are all these questions important?" In the beginning, the students had asked any question, no matter how obvious or trivial. Together they weeded out any that didn't seem important, and from that point on, her students worked to ask only questions that were thoughtful and related to the big issues in the story, rather than questions about trivial details. When the students began asking better questions during read-aloud, Joyce had them practice the strategy in their independent reading.

FIGURE 5.1 Bethany's *Ramona's World* chart

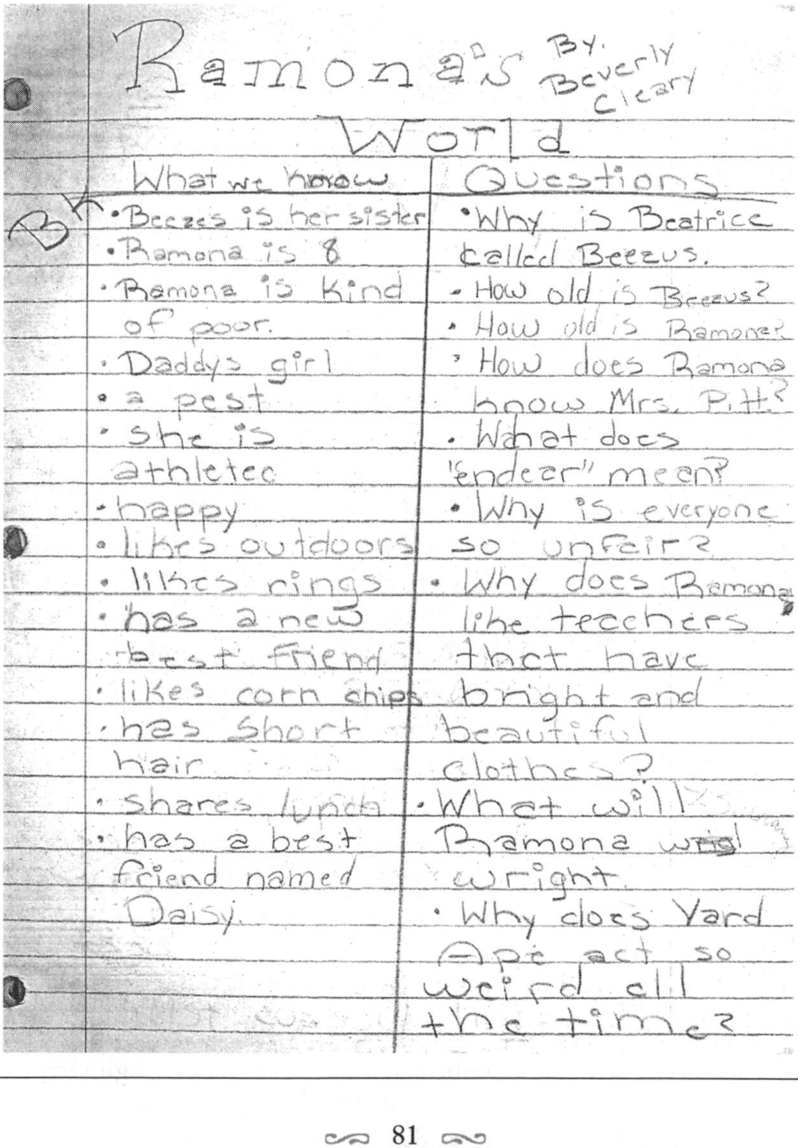
Ramona's World
By. Beverly Cleary

What we know	Questions
• Beezes is her sister	• Why is Beatrice called Beezus.
• Ramona is 8	• How old is Beezus?
• Ramona is kind of poor.	• How old is Ramona?
• Daddys girl	• How does Ramona know Mrs. Pitt?
• a pest	• What does "endear" mean?
• she is athletec	• Why is everyone so unfair?
• happy	• Why does Ramona like teechers that have bright and beautiful clothes?
• likes outdoors	• What will Ramona wright.
• likes rings	• Why does Yard Ape act so weird all the time?
• has a new best friend	
• likes corn chips	
• has short hair	
• shares lunch	
• has a best friend named Daisy.	

This focus on thoughtful, important questioning that began during read-aloud paid off later in the year in health when Joyce's students were brainstorming research questions about body systems. She was impressed by the depth and quality of their questions—tangible evidence that they had internalized what she had taught and could apply it in a new situation.

Text-to-Text Connections

Sometimes the text-to-text connections during read-aloud happen spontaneously, but sometimes you can deliberately choose a book that will guarantee connections. When my students were studying mythology in the library with our media specialist, I chose to read aloud *It's All Greek to Me* by Jon Scieszka.

Even though I thought I knew what would happen with the connections, there were still plenty of surprises. The first came when we were previewing the book and studying the cover illustration. Kyle, a devoted Harry Potter fan, shouted, "Fluffy!" when he saw Cerebrus, the three-headed dog, on the cover. Earlier in the year, just before the Harry Potter movie came out, I had brought in an article from *USA Today* that told about characters and situations that J. K. Rowling had borrowed from mythology and other sources. The article was still hanging on a clip below the chalkboard, so I took it out and read it to them again. Now that they were learning about the mythological characters, the connections to Harry Potter were much clearer. When we got to the part in the book where the characters discover that music will calm the beasts, Kyle again made the connection to Harry, Ron, and Hermione calming Fluffy with music. One of the students, who belongs to my parent/child book club, made a connection to the way William uses music to calm the beasts in the forest in *The Castle in the Attic* by Elizabeth Winthrop, our previous book club book. Mythology—Harry Potter—*USA Today*—*The Castle in the Attic*. I hadn't planned on *those* connections!

Tsilat has been reading mythology on her own since at least the beginning of the year and perhaps longer. She made the kind of connections I was expecting—recognizing the mythological characters in *It's All Greek to Me* by name or symbol or personality. Even though I was expecting this kind of connection, Tsilat still amazed me. She would fill in the names of gods and goddess as I read. "A gorgeous woman leading a peacock—"

"Hera!"

Or "We stared at the incredible thrones. Each was different. The biggest one had an emblem of an eagle clutching jagged thunderbolts."

"Zeus!"

"The throne next to it was covered with carvings of horse heads and waves."

"Poseidon!"

Any time Jon Scieszka gave the reader a clue about a god or goddess without giving the name, Tsilat could supply it. Based on her knowledge of mythological characters, she even accurately predicted the solution to the problem of Sam knowing how to play only one song—"Twinkle, Twinkle, Little Star"—on his lyre at the end of the book when the characters needed to calm all the fighting gods and goddesses on Mount Olympus. "If only we could find someone who could play more," I read. "But who . . . ?"

"Apollo, god of music!" Tsilat blurted gleefully as I took a breath before reading on: "'Apollo,' said a voice in my ear."

Tsilat and several others began independently reading some of the other Time Warp Trio books. During that time, the topic for their short daily responses for their Reading at Home assignment was, not surprisingly, connections, and again she and the others surpassed my simple expectation of connections between mythological characters and *It's All Greek to Me* by making text-to-text connections between the various Time Warp Trio books and to the Magic Tree House series.

This experience of having my expectations surpassed in so many different ways reminded me of the importance of following my students' lead. It is ludicrous to believe that my way is always the best or right way.

Historical Facts

In the middle grades, students begin to develop a sense of history, to collect historical facts, and to create a mental time line to keep history straight, at least in terms of before this and after that, if not yet by exact dates.

It has been my experience that students do not fall in love with learning about history by reading their social studies textbook. It is the story in history (or herstory, for that matter) that hooks a learner. It might be the stories that parents or grandparents tell, or movies set in a time period or that tell the story of a historical event, or books of historical fiction, but it is the story that begins a casual or passionate lifelong pursuit of history.

We can support this growing understanding of and passion for history by including historical fiction in our read-alouds, and by making it a point to help differentiate between historical fact and fiction.

Fourth-grade teacher Joyce Zawaly uses *Trace Through the Forest* by Barbara Robinson to make the years of the early settlement of Ohio come to life for her students. As she reads, her students make connections to the factual information they've read in their social studies books. Sometimes they even go back to their social studies book to check the historic accuracy of *Trace Through the Forest*.

When I read *Weasel* to my fourth graders, one of my goals, like Joyce's, is to make early Ohio history come to life. To help my students begin to be able to differentiate fact from fiction, we keep a two-column chart labeled "History" and "Fiction" to which we add each time we read.

Our fifth graders study American history and begin to read more and more historical fiction. Julia Barthelmes has found that when she reads aloud *The Witch of Blackbird Pond* by Elizabeth George Speare early in the year, it introduces her fifth graders to aspects of daily life in Colonial America to which they return throughout the year in social studies. Not only that, but the early focus on the historical lays the groundwork for her students' independent reading of historical fiction throughout the year.

Trust the Author

It's been several years since I've read aloud *The True Confessions of Charlotte Doyle* by Avi. I love this book, but it won't work as a read-aloud with every class. Your class must absolutely and completely trust that you will choose great read-alouds. They must be patient listeners—for half a book, not just for one or two read-aloud sessions. It's not until the second half that the action and adventure starts. *Charlotte Doyle* also works best if you have a class maybe not entirely composed of, but at least liberally sprinkled with, readers who are ready to read longer, more complicated fiction.

From the very first day I read *Charlotte Doyle*, I talked to my students about trusting Avi, the author. I warned them that the first half of the book would seem slow, but told them that I had no doubt that they would believe it was all worth it when we got to the second half. Throughout the first half of the book, rather than just letting them whine about how slow the story was going and how dull Charlotte was, I guided my students to question why Avi had chosen to pace the story that way, and to look for Charlotte's not-so-obvious qualities. We looked for hints of what might happen in the second half of the story, and we continually speculated about the "Important Warning" at the beginning of the book: "Not every thirteen-year-old girl is accused of murder, brought to trial, and found guilty. But I was just such a girl, and my story is worth relating even if it did happen years ago . . ." (p. 1).

No matter how much groundwork you lay, nothing can adequately prepare your students for the shift that takes place midway through this book. Their surprise and delight when the book changes from a smotheringly slow stroll into a galloping romp proves to them more than any lesson you can devise that it is worth it to trust the author through the slow parts, because there could be no exciting parts without them.

Read-Aloud Props

One of the reasons it is necessary to read every read-aloud prior to reading it to your class is that you can be on the lookout for props to make the book come alive for your students.

I can't imagine reading *Walk Two Moons* (Creech) without having a write-on/wipe-off map of the United States handy so that the class can keep track of the route Salamanca and her grandparents take to Idaho.

Music is important in *The Watson's Go to Birmingham—1963* (Curtis). I had just about given up on finding the songs "Yakety-Yak" and "Under the Boardwalk" at the public library when Amanda brought in her mom's collection of cassettes of oldies. I copied both songs onto my own cassette, and now I will have them handy every time I read *The Watsons*.

Disney made a movie of the story of Ruby Bridges that our fifth graders watched after hearing *The Story of Ruby Bridges* by Robert Coles and *Through My Eyes* by Ruby Bridges. I try not to overdo movie-book comparisons. For one thing, I believe that the book is always better than the movie. And since it is more likely that a child will experience the movie version than the book version at home, I choose to emphasize the book and leave the movie watching to their free time at home.

It's always fun to eat a food that is featured in a book. Peaches are rarely in season when I'm ready to read aloud *James and the Giant Peach* (Dahl), so next time I read it we'll have to make do with the token peach pits I cleaned and dried after a summer peach-picking escapade. Most often when I share a food from the book we've read, it is with my student/parent book club, since it would become far too expensive to do for the whole class for every read-aloud. In fact, it is a ritual of our book club to begin the discussion by speculating what the snack could be. Kaitlyn and her mom went so far as to keep a list—with page numbers—of every food mentioned in each book we read. I had to be very creative to surprise them. One student/parent book club had Oreos and milk from *Tales of a Fourth Grade Nothing* (Blume), just juice (literally) from *Just Juice* (Hesse), apples from *The Castle in the Attic* (Winthrop), figs from *The Battle for the Castle* (Winthrop), Pop Rocks candy (fireworks for our mouths) from *The Firework-Maker's Daughter* (Pullman), and gummy fish from *Island of the Blue Dolphins* (O'Dell).

Copy the diagram of the ship and the information on the ringing of the ship's bells that are included in the book for your students to study while you read *The True Confessions of Charlotte Doyle*. For those who are not familiar with the parts of a two-masted sailing ship from the early 1800s (i.e., most or all of your students), this will provide a support for understanding the sailing terminology that Avi weaves into the story.

You couldn't plan for this one, but it is a testimonial to being flexible and spontaneous and ready for any teaching opportunity that presents itself. I had decided to have a little music playing in the background while the students worked on their pictures of a character and a scene from *It's All Greek to Me*. I held up two CDs and asked, "Which would you rather hear, six- and twelve-string guitar by Leo Kottke, or different variations of Pachelbel's Canon in D?" It was a rhetorical question. I knew it was likely that none of them would ever choose to hear either CD. In his best "you are so weird, but we'll humor you" voice, John said, "You decide, Ms. Hahn." Then the inspiration came to me in a flash. I had to play the Pachelbel variations because in *It's All Greek to Me*, Apollo plays variations of "Twinkle, Twinkle, Little Star" to calm the out-of-control gods, goddesses, and monsters in the fight scene. A perfect musical connection . . . by accident!

Rereading

How the Study Came to Be

It is painful to admit that I am still occasionally guilty of skipping the important middle phases of the Apprenticeship Model. I go directly from modeling to expecting my students to independently use what I've shown them, without the support of either shared or guided practice. It happened recently when I began to look closely at rereading to try to discover why this important habit was not a bigger part of my students' reading lives.

At the end of every read-aloud, we linger with the book for a day or more, identifying favorite parts, rereading, and talking, talking, talking. So why, I wondered, when my students are finished reading a book, do they slam it shut and immediately go look for another? The ritual of the birthday read-aloud sends us back over and over again to favorite books. So why, I wondered, are my students so averse to books they've already read?

The answer was obvious as soon as I asked the questions. I needed to completely teach these two habits, rather than just modeling them and then expecting the students to use them independently. I planned an eight-day unit of study on lingering and rereading for reading workshop that would be anchored by the modeling of lingering and rereading I had done in read-aloud, but would provide the students with the critical elements of shared and guided practice using the books they were reading or had read.

I planned this study around the question, "What does it do for a reader to linger with a book when she's finished, or reread a favorite book or a favorite part of a book?" In short, "Why reread?" There was no content information to be disseminated in this unit of study. Although I had a few premises or observations I would share to get us started, I set out intending to learn as much or more than my students. I knew that my learning, as much as my teaching, would follow where they led.

My first premise was that a reader rereads or lingers to revisit favorite books or favorite parts of a book. I took this premise directly from my own life. One of my favorite Sunday afternoon activities as a child was to reread a book that would make me cry, such as *Little Britches* by Ralph Moody, or *Love Story* by Erich Segal, or *Old Yeller* by Fred Gipson. I was (and am) amazed that authors could move me to tears with their words. I also see that revisiting favorite parts is important when I consider the kinds of choices my students make for their birthday read-aloud. Go's choice for his birthday read-aloud was the parts of *Because of Winn-Dixie* (DiCamillo) where we learn that Otis has been to jail and how he got there. Then, after I had read those, someone requested the part where Otis brings the pickles to the party. And even if Jessica hadn't asked, I would have reread the list of ten things about India Opal's mother and the list of ten things about Winn-Dixie. Once we got started, we almost couldn't stop rereading our favorite parts!

Another of my initial premises was that readers reread or linger to make more sense of a confusing part or because they understand more or discover more on the second read. I recently reread *The Giver* (Lowry) so that I could discuss the ending with a friend. I was surprised at all the parts I had forgotten, and I surprised her with my new theories about what that sled ride at the end could mean. I also saw this discovery of more meaning happen with Caitlyn's birthday read-aloud (Dav Pilkey's *Dogzilla*), and John's birthday read-aloud (David Weisner's *The Three Pigs*). It was almost as though the first read had been for enjoyment and the second was for analysis. On the second reads, the class carefully studied each page and throughout both books made discoveries in the illustrations and in the text that they had missed the first time.

My final premise seemed true mostly for rereading or lingering specifically with a read-aloud. Based on my observations during read-aloud, I sometimes had the sense that the first read had been a practice, and the second (or third, or more) read was a performance. Becca's birthday read-aloud was *Baloney (Henry P.)* (Scieszka). One of the things she loved about this book was all the words in different languages, and she admitted that she had studied the promotional poster that hangs on the word wall by the sink when she was getting a drink or washing her hands. Many of the students chimed in that they, too, had studied the poster while at the sink. The spoonerism *sighing flosser* for *flying saucer* had made a big impression. Earlier in the day I had been telling stories about my days as a lifeguard, so I told the students about the spoonerisms that my fellow guards and I had made with each other's names. Of course, then we had to make each student's name into a spoonerism. Once we were finished with spoonerisms and I started reading the book, I could tell that they had, indeed, been studying the poster over the sink. When I came to the words that are not in English, such as Henry's trusty *zimulus*, I could hear quiet voices giving the translation, *pencil*. Read-aloud that day had a definite feel of performance to it. The first read and the poster had taught the students their "lines," and the students delightfully participated in the reread.

This sense of reread as performance came again with *It's All Greek to Me*. For his birthday read-aloud, Ethan chose the part of *It's All Greek to Me* where Sam and Hera trade insults back and forth. This would be my third reading of that chapter.

The first time I read that part, I could tell the insults were going right past my students. I paused after Hera asks, "Are you paying attention?" and Sam answers, "I did once, but it wouldn't pay me back." I waited for some laughter, but they just looked at me. I began stopping after each insult, either to explain it, or simply to give the humor enough time to soak in.

> "Maybe you can help me out."
>
> "We'd love to help you out," said Sam. "Which way did you come in?"
>
> "One of us is crazy. But don't worry, I'll keep your secret," answered Hera with her own insult.
>
> "Where have you been all my life? And when are you going back there?" countered Sam.
>
> Hera gave another laugh. "How can I miss you when you won't go away?"
>
> Sam grinned. "I never forget a face, but in your case, I'll make an exception."
>
> Hera howled, laughing so hard she was crying.
>
> Sam added another. "You have a face like a baby, and a mind to match."

At the end of that chapter, Joe hears "the sound of marching feet." The first time I read it, I invited the students to do the sound effects with their feet. Joe also hears the sound of "one voice calling, the others answering" and again I invited the students to help:

> "We are monsters, we are tough," I sang as if I were a drill sergeant.

"WE ARE MONSTERS, WE ARE TOUGH," the students sang back. And on we went, with me helping out on the response when it wasn't simply the repeat of what I had sung.

"We don't take nobody's guff."

"WE DON'T TAKE NOBODY'S GUFF"

"Sound off!"

"MON-STERS!"

"Say it again!"

"MON-STERS!"

"Bring it on down!"

"MONSTERS, MONSTERS, MONSTERS"

"WE RULE!"

The next day, Nicole asked if we could start back at the insults and *then* read on. The second time around, everyone laughed in all the right places, the marching started as if on cue, and the monsters' chant was sung with gusto. It was as if the first read had been a rehearsal.

The third time, for Ethan's birthday read-aloud, it was even more like a performance. This time, students were not just laughing at the insults, but chiming in and saying them along with me as I read.

The Unit of Study

The night before I began the unit of study, I gathered a bag of books for rereading that I would use to model the steps for book selection and reflective thinking that I wanted my students to practice. First, I looked back over my list of books read to find potential titles. I chose *Girl with a Pearl Earring* by Tracy Chevalier because I wanted to reread the examples of rich language that I had highlighted. Then I browsed my shelves. Among the books I chose were *Little Britches* (Moody) because I wondered if the ending could still make me cry (I tested it when I took it off the shelf—it could), the McDuff stories by Rosemary Wells because I wanted to enjoy again Susan Jeffers's illustrations of West Highland white terriers, and *It's Not About the Bike* by Lance Armstrong so I could work on a sticky note project that I had started back when I first read a library copy of the book.

I began the unit by gathering my students in our meeting area and explaining why we were going to do this short study. I told them I was curious about why I had never seen any of them rereading, even after we had reread together after every read-aloud and for birthday read-alouds. On a sheet of chart paper, I wrote the core question for the study, "Why reread?" and together we brainstormed some initial ideas. The first reason given was that good readers reread a little of the previous chapter before reading on in their book so that they can remember what was happening. I was pleased that the students had internalized this habit for remembering where they left off, but it wasn't the rereading habit I was looking for. I redirected their thinking by saying, "What about rereading after you are finished with a book?" We added two more items to the chart: to understand better (confusing parts), and to get more out of it (remembering things you'd forgotten or noticing things you hadn't noticed the first time).

Next, I shared my bag of books with them and explained the steps I had followed to decide what I would reread. We talked about them using their list of books read to choose rereads, and how browsing the shelves might help. I showed them how highlighting or turning down corners in a book of my own helped me reread favorite parts, and how the extensive sticky notes I had placed in a library book helped me decide to buy the book for myself. I had put the page number and a short note on each sticky note and saved them in the back of my literature log, and I wanted to reread so I could put them into my copy of the book.

I asked the students to log the rereading they did each day by noting the title and author of the book or books they reread, and by writing a short reflection on the power or purpose of their rereading that day. At the end of each reading period, we would come back together and share, and add any new thoughts to our "Why reread?" chart.

When I sent them off to read that first day, many went straight to their list of books read or to our gallery of read-alouds to gather titles. Some went straight to a particular book, and the rest spread out to browse at different bookshelves in different areas of the room—some at picture books, some at poetry and fairy tales, some at easy books, and some at the tubs of books in the classroom library. There was lots of quiet conversation as students made their choices and offered suggestions. As they settled down to read, I circulated and chatted with some of them about their books.

Eric was feeling like he had ESP; just the day before, he had checked out a book he had read early in the year so that he could reread it. One of the most avid readers in the class was rereading a book from home that she had in her backpack—a book she had already reread at least five times. These were my first hints that perhaps my assumption that my students didn't reread independently might be false.

Some students chose books to reread in their entirety, whereas others were selectively rereading parts of a book—usually the funny parts. When I saw that Nicole was rereading the insults in *It's All Greek to Me*, I asked her what it was like to read them yet again. They weren't as funny as the first couple of times, she admitted. "The first time, we didn't even get them until you explained them. The second time they were really funny. The third time they were sort of funny, but now they are kind of boring."

In the first few days of the study when we got together to share after reading, we added two more ideas to our "Why reread?" chart: because it's a good book—a favorite—and because it was a read-aloud and you

FIGURE 5.2 Ashley's rereading *Because of Winn-Dixie* by Kate DiCamillo

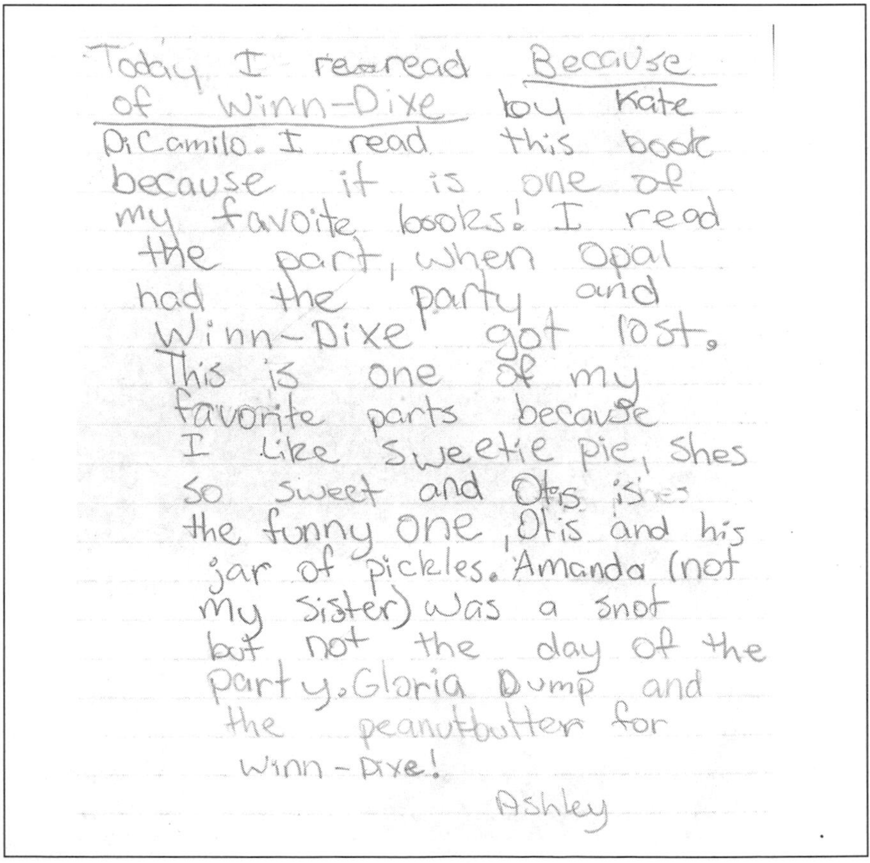

Today I re-read Because of Winn-Dixe by Kate DiCamilo. I read this book because it is one of my favorite books! I read the part, when Opal had the party, and Winn-Dixie got lost. This is one of my favorite parts because I like Sweetie pie, Shes so sweet and Otis is the funny one, Otis and his jar of pickles. Amanda (not my sister) was a snot but not the day of the party. Gloria Dump and the peanutbutter for Winn-Dixe!

Ashley

want to read it for yourself. Although there were students such as Shane, who deliberately went back to the very first book they had read that year, no one saw rereading as a form of self-evaluation to test how far they had come in their reading. For the most part, we kept going back to the basic ideas on the chart—we reread favorite books or favorite parts to enjoy them again, to get more out of the book, to remember parts we had forgotten, and to understand parts that were confusing the first time.

After the study was completed and I read over their logs, I was impressed by Ashley's and Beth's detailed descriptions of the parts they had chosen to reread and why (see Figures 5.2 and 5.3). Beth even

FIGURE 5.3 Beth's rereading

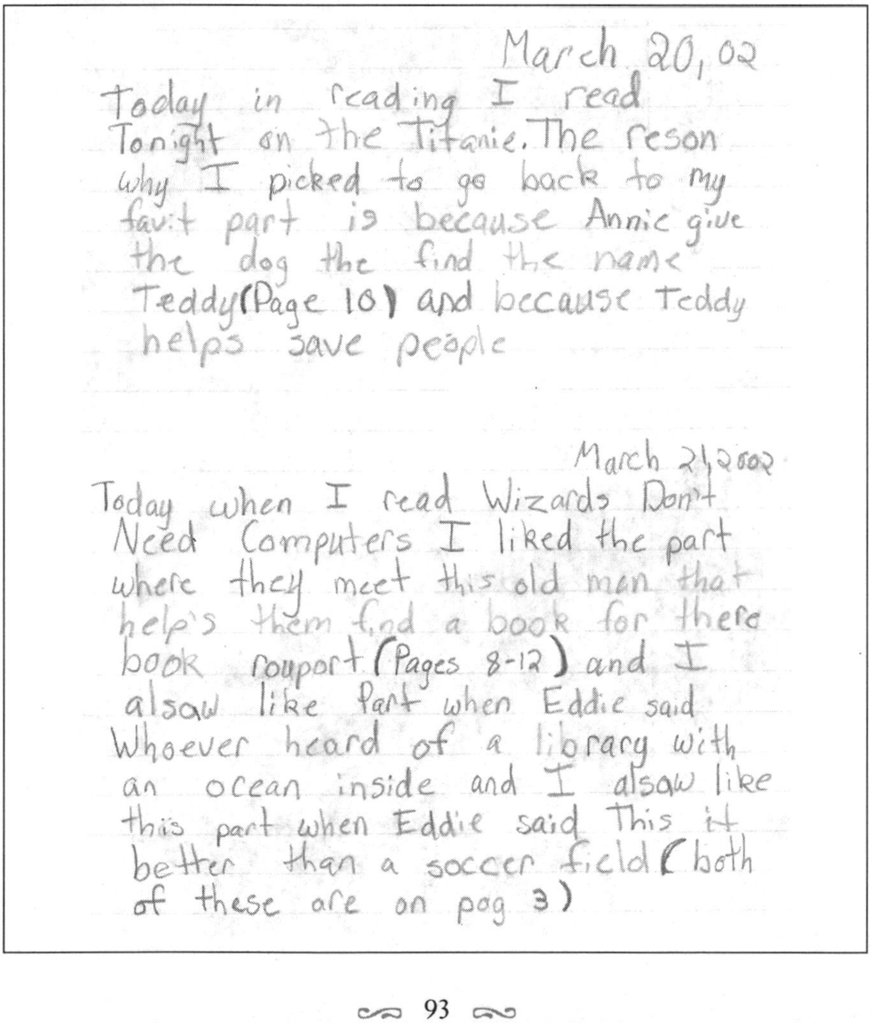

> March 20, 02
> Today in reading I read Tonight on the Titanic. The reson why I picked to go back to my favit part is because Annie give the dog the find the name Teddy (Page 10) and because Teddy helps save people
>
> March 21 2002
> Today when I read Wizards Don't Need Computers I liked the part where they meet this old man that help's them find a book for there book rouport (Pages 8-12) and I alsow like Part when Eddie said Whoever heard of a library with an ocean inside and I alsow like this part when Eddie said This it better than a soccer field (both of these are on pog 3)

included the page numbers. Almost everyone enjoyed rereading and most could imagine doing it again in the future. Marissa wrote, "I think we should reread some books every other week." One student wrote, "I don't really like it but I think other people do. I haven't read many books so I had to read the same books over." Perhaps, I thought, he understands now why I made him agree to wait to read the fourth Harry Potter until summer vacation. Nicole's concluding thoughts were "How it felt . . . oh that is hard. It went so well I can't even tell—it was super de-duper good. Rereading is now my favorite thing to do. I might even still be rereading. I already have been to at least 100–130 books. I like rereading because it feels like I'm really in the book. Maybe because I understand it more. Well, that's all."

Our study is completed, but in future reading conferences with my students, I will be sure to ask them about their rereading habits as I continue to gather anecdotal data on the question "Why reread?"

∽ 6 ∽
Nonfiction Strategies

If our goal is to develop whole readers, nonfiction must get equal time in read-aloud. Most children have had a steady diet of fiction read-alouds, from the time they were babies (if they were lucky) and all through school. By hearing stories again and again, they have developed an innate sense for the structure of a fictional story—characters in a setting, with a plot that involves some kind of conflict, and action that builds to a climax and/or resolution. Nonfiction has a very different structure. Children must learn to listen for such structures as main ideas and supporting examples, ideas that are compared and contrasted, causes and effects, and events in chronological order. By hearing nonfiction again and again, they can develop an innate sense for the structure of a nonfiction text. This will benefit the intermediate student not only as a listener, but as a reader who will more and more frequently be required to learn by reading nonfiction.

Teachers need to be experienced readers of nonfiction who are able to identify nonfiction's structures, and they need to be intentional in their inclusion of nonfiction in the read-aloud. After that, there is no formula or script for the instructional choices an experienced reader of nonfiction makes when sharing an interesting and/or topical text. It is a dance between the teacher, who knows what she could teach, and the text, which provides the opportunities. It is only necessary to maintain a balance between interrupted read-aloud (direct instruction) and noninterrupted read-aloud (enjoyment, learning, and practice listening for the structure).

Choosing a Nonfiction Read-Aloud

I had three nonfiction books in mind for the next read-aloud. Each one had been a successful nonfiction read-aloud in previous years: *Autumn Across America* by Seymour Simon, *While a Tree Was Growing* by Jane Bosveld, and *One World, Many Religions* by Mary Pope Osborne. *Autumn Across America* would be a perfect text-to-world connection because the trees were in full color. *While a Tree Was Growing* would give my history buffs a different viewpoint of history—a view centering on the natural world rather than on military conflicts. And now, more than ever, I knew the class needed to learn the information and have the discussions that *One World, Many Religions* would provide.

Modeling Book Selection

Rather than choosing the next read-aloud myself, I used this opportunity to model the habit (plague?) of having several books in mind to read next, and let the class work through the decision-making process. I previewed each book and told why I thought it would be the perfect one to read next. Then I let them vote. *Autumn Across America* got one vote, and the rest of the students wanted to hear *One World, Many Religions*. Another year, that choice might have surprised me. But the world has changed, right down to its youngest citizens. These children now feel an intense desire and an urgent necessity to understand "others" and find out what makes us "us." At the core of their search is the need to learn what causes cultures to hate one another.

On the second day, before I began reading aloud, I tested my assumptions about why they had nearly unanimously chosen this book for read-aloud. "What made you want to hear this book most of all?" I asked.

"To learn about different cultures," Kyle answered without hesitation. "Actually, I have two," he said. "Also to learn about what you have in you." Just what I had thought: finding out about others and about themselves. Other students hoped to learn how many different religions there are, how other religions work, and how they got started. Basic information gathering. One student wanted to find out how other religions celebrate Christ. This comment gave me a glimpse of all the possible misconceptions nine- and ten-year-olds might have about religion. Ideally, by the end of the book, he would understand that each religion celebrates its own holy people. In its egocentrism, his statement revealed one reason cultures hate one another—each believes its religion is the one true religion. It is not the purpose of Osborne's book, nor was it my purpose in reading this book aloud, to explore the truth of any religion, and certainly not to extol any religion over another. In *One World, Many Religions*, Osborne provides a balance beam of factual information about religions, upon which I carefully trod as I read this book aloud. I hoped that, by the end of the book, armed with facts with which to form opinions and make generalizations, the students could begin to infer on their own that no matter what forms they take, all religions are true because they are true to the ones who believe in them.

The First Nonfiction Book of the Year

My purpose for reading aloud *One World, Many Religions* was many-layered. Along with the community building, the talk about a big topic, and the multicultural understandings, I read it to begin to teach my students to hear the structures of nonfiction. To determine where they were in their development as listeners to nonfiction, I asked one more question before I began reading again on the second day. "What is different about listening to a nonfiction read-aloud?" Blank stares. "What's different about what goes on inside your head while you listen?" A few hands were tentatively raised.

"The pictures I make in my mind are more real."

"I have to listen more closely to the facts."

Rather than feeling discouraged about how little they knew and/or how much they needed the language to describe what they knew about listening to nonfiction and about nonfiction structures, I made a mental note to ask this question again at the end of the book to see how far they had come. I'll ask it again at the beginning and end of each nonfiction book throughout our time together to measure their growth, my teaching, and the power of the nonfiction read-aloud.

Topic Sentences

When I read this sentence, I knew that Osborne had given me my lesson on nonfiction structures for the day's read-aloud: "But since the 1800s Judaism has branched into three large groups: Orthodox, Reform, and Conservative Judaism." I told the students that a sentence like that was a clue from the author that she or he would be telling the reader about those three groups in the paragraphs that followed. "Listen carefully, and when you hear me reading about Orthodox Judaism, raise one finger. When I switch to Reform, raise two fingers. And when you hear me read about Conservative, raise three fingers," I said.

Clues in the Text When the Topic Changes

After that section, there was a wide break in the text, which I pointed out to the students. "The author has given us a clue for our eyes that she is going to write about a different topic next. Listen to this sentence and see if you can tell what her new topic is: 'For centuries, holidays and traditions have been an essential part of Jewish life.'" I didn't get the answering chorus of "Holidays and traditions!" so I made a mental note that on another day, the lesson would be to listen carefully for topic sentences and main ideas.

Main Idea

Before the first snow, and before the solstice brought the official beginning of winter, I read aloud *Autumn Across America*. Simon's books generally follow the same format. Each two-page spread has one page of text on one or two topics and a beautiful full-color photograph that relates to the text, sometimes more, sometimes less. After reading the first page, I modeled a comprehension strategy. I thought aloud about what the main ideas on that page had been, jotted a quick note on a sticky note that I placed on the page, and read on. After modeling the strategy for several pages, I asked for student input on the main ideas. The next day in read-aloud, I had each student take out two or three sticky notes. At the end of each page I read, I asked the students to turn to a partner and come up with the sticky note they would write for the main idea of that page. The last day of reading aloud *Autumn Across America* I didn't want to interrupt the flow of the reading as much as the partner sticky notes had, so I planned to go back to modeling the sticky note strategy while the students just listened. However, Marissa was prepared to work without being asked—she already had three big sticky notes out on her desk. I thanked her for being prepared, and explained that I intended to do all the work that day. "But can we write the sticky notes if we want to?" begged Becca. How could I say no? And so Marissa, Becca, Caitlyn, Amanda, and Tori contributed the sticky notes for the last few pages of the book.

Several days later, after giving instructions for an activity, I asked, "Who can sum up what I just said?" Then I added, in an unplanned but brilliant world-to-text connection: "If you could put a sticky note on the page of what I just said, what would your sticky note say?" With that question, giving and receiving directions became a quick follow-up lesson on determining the main idea.

A Nonfiction Study That Is Anchored in Read-Aloud

Third-grade teacher Karen Terlecky has worked for several years to refine and perfect her nonfiction unit. In the past, she did a biography unit and was naïve enough to call it her nonfiction unit.

Her current unit bears little resemblance to those early units. Her teaching is strategy-based, wisely planned, and anchored in her read-aloud. Long before she teaches her nonfiction unit, she teaches the strategy of questioning, which will be a fundamental skill in studying and learning from nonfiction. She models the strategy during read-aloud with fiction first. Her students work with questioning in shared and guided activities, and finally, use it independently with the books they are reading.

Before the nonfiction unit, Karen also teaches her students to write clear and concise summaries—"the essence of report writing," she says. Again, she begins her teaching cycle for this skill with modeling using her fiction read-aloud. Karen times her nonfiction unit for the second semester of third grade. Knowing the kinds of skills she will be expecting of her students, she does not believe they would be ready for her nonfiction unit in second grade, and not even in the first half of third grade.

Once she is ready to launch her nonfiction unit, Karen makes room in her schedule for two read-alouds per day. She maintains a fiction read-aloud, because she knows that when she asks her students to do all of their independent reading at school in nonfiction, it will be important to maintain a story as a break so they don't burn out. Her nonfiction read-aloud becomes a teaching tool for modeling questioning and summarizing with nonfiction, as well as a myriad of other skills. Karen has found the Ranger Rick Big Books published by Newbridge to be invaluable resources for her nonfiction read-alouds.

One of Karen's first goals is to have her students understand the range of books that constitute nonfiction (animals, sports, biographies and autobiographies, weather, cultures, geography, etc.) and to acquaint them with all the nonfiction in their classroom library. For one session early in the unit her class simply sits in a circle and passes books around, browsing in each one for a minute or less before passing it on. Karen also is careful to read aloud from a variety of nonfiction books.

Another important goal is that her students become familiar with nonfiction characteristics such as graphs, maps, pictures and captions, and so on. After identifying each of the characteristics in read-aloud, each student makes a poster of several nonfiction characteristics and includes information on why each is necessary in the nonfiction book in which it was found.

Finally, Karen's students are ready to apply all they have learned about nonfiction. Each student chooses a topic for an Interest Investigation. This is the first time most of them have written a report, but because Karen has carefully planned their nonfiction study, they are equipped with the skills that will ensure their success. They choose their resources wisely, ask important, thoughtful questions, summarize their reading without copying from the book, and create a final project that incorporates four or five nonfiction characteristics. It's pretty impressive for third graders, but a natural extension of all of the wisely planned teaching Karen has done—teaching that is anchored in her read-aloud.

Evaluation
and Assessment

The words *assessment* and *evaluation* are sometimes used interchangeably. But evaluation, which means to determine or set the value of a thing, has a more final ring to it than assessment, which means to estimate, judge, review, or consider. In education, evaluation comes at the end of a period of learning, whereas assessment is what drives teaching and learning. Evaluation determines how things turned out in the end, but continuous assessment is what guided you there.

Evaluating Read-Aloud

There are less than twenty days of school remaining. It seems like a lifetime ago that I sat on the classroom floor in front of my picture-book shelves with a shoe box, picking first read-alouds for a classroom full of imaginary students. From this vantage point, I can evaluate the successes of this year's read-aloud.

We have become a community of readers. Read-aloud has given us books and characters and authors in common from the very first day of school, and we have built our classroom community around books. My students have Sponge Bob Square Pants and I have classical guitar music, but together we've got books. We keep piles of books at our desks, share favorite authors and discover new favorites, recommend books to each other, beg to be the next one to read a "hot" book, and debate about the characters or situations in books. The common language in my classroom is the language of books.

My students love reading. Michelle's mom was recently surprised and pleased when Michelle chose to read instead of watching TV one morning before school. A day or two later, Michelle came to me with a "problem." She was next on the list to read the twenty-fifth Magic Tree House book, but she was very involved in Gordon Korman's Island series *and* she still needed to finish *Music of the Dolphins* (Hesse) for book club. She wondered if we could skip her for the Magic Tree House book and come back to her later. Ten years old and she already understands the saying "So many books, so little time."

My students love read-aloud. Kyle is still struggling to break free of Harry Potter. Exasperated with my book recommendations, he finally told me to just pick books for him like the ones I read aloud, because he always loves them. One of the class's current favorite read-alouds is *The True Confessions of Charlotte Doyle* (Avi). Jessica, whose picture could be in the dictionary next to the entry for "dog lover," unhesitatingly put *Charlotte Doyle* ahead of *Because of Winn-Dixie* (DiCamillo) for her favorite read-aloud of the year . . . and then reversed the decision a few weeks later. Nicole followed along in her own book when I read *The True Confessions of Charlotte Doyle.* When Captain Jaggery flogs Zachariah, Nicole, her hand over her mouth and her eyes glued to the page, said, "Oh! This is *not* G rated! . . . Keep reading!" And in an interviewing activity for Drug Abuse Resistance Education (D.A.R.E.), Amanda asked

Caitlyn, "If you could be any character in a book, who would you be?" (Great question.) Caitlyn's answer? Charlotte Doyle. (Great answer.)

Assessing Read-Aloud

Assessment happens when we watch and listen. Assessment is informal and anecdotal.

Watch

I sometimes assess story comprehension out of the corner of my eye during read-aloud. During *Weasel* (DeFelice), when I read, "Pa pushed his lower lip out and pulled on his whiskers like he did sometimes when he was working on an idea," I caught a quick glimpse of several students pulling on imaginary whiskers with their lower lip pushed out. In *Because of Winn-Dixie*, whenever I read about the Preacher rubbing his nose, several students were rubbing their noses, too. When the Christmas Knight in *Christmas in Camelot* (Osborne) pointed his red-gloved hand at Jack and Annie to send them to the Otherworld to recapture Camelot's joy, hands all around the room were pointing. And when the Christmas Knight raised his hand and froze all of Camelot in time, hands all around the room were raised.

Listen

I listen closely to my students during read-aloud to assess their comprehension of the story. When they laugh out loud, or when they cry, I know they understand the story deeply. Sometimes they make quiet little "comments" that don't interrupt the reading at all, but let me know they completely understand: "Eeewww," "gross," "cool," "a-ha," or "uh-oh." They "talk back to the text," saying things such as, "Yeah, right," "That could never happen," or, about a character's actions, "That was *cold*."

When my students interrupt my reading to ask the meaning of a word, or to ask a question, I know they are working hard to comprehend the story, and I don't mind stopping to answer them, or to put their question out to the class for everyone to think about and answer. During those times when I have been interrupted and I stop reading for a minute or two, it seems like we have hit an imaginary "pause" button in the story. We take a minute or two for conversation or to clear up some confusion, and then hit the pause button once more to resume action of the story.

Sometimes when I listen to my students outside of read-aloud, I hear conversations that never could have happened if it weren't for read-aloud. I listened in on a discussion that David, Nicole, Preet, Tsilat, and Becca were having in their literature circle. They had just finished reading *The Sign of the Beaver* (Speare), and they immediately connected the book to an earlier read-aloud, Weasel, and launched into a point-by-point comparison of the two books.

Whenever I hear the words "I've got a connection!" I know a reading strategy that I first taught during read-aloud is being applied in some new way or in some new situation. Recently, when I was reading *So Far from the Sea* by Eve Bunting in preparation for the visit of illustrator Chris Soentpiet to our school, the description of the father's reaction to the child asking why the father and other relatives had been relocated to Manzanar caused gasps of recognition and connection: "Dad pulls his head far back into his hood, like a snail going into a shell." In *Because of Winn-Dixie*, Kate DiCamillo describes the Preacher as pulling into himself like a turtle pulling into its shell.

Informal

Even when I assess my students' understanding of or response to read-aloud in a paper-and-pencil kind of way, I work hard to make it informal. Last year's class wrote persuasive letters to convince me of what the next read-aloud should be. My end-of-year read-aloud survey has just four questions: What's your favorite thing about read-aloud? What happens inside your brain during read-aloud? Did you learn anything about reading during read-aloud that you used during your own reading? and What else did you learn during read-aloud? I was away at a conference for almost all of *Be a Perfect Person in Just Three Days* (Manes) this year, so when I returned, I asked my students to write me a letter telling me what they thought of the book. When we finished *Meet Addy* (Porter), I asked my students to write me a letter or an essay addressing these questions: "Why do you think it's important to read about history? How does it make you feel to learn about the Civil War and about slavery? Do you think *Meet Addy* was well written? Why or why not? What historical period do you think it would be interesting to write about? Why? What would you write? From whose point of view?"

One thing sometimes leads to another with assessment. Besides being interested in what my students had to say in their answers to the *Meet Addy* questions, I was interested to learn how many of them did not know what a "historical period" was. Julia Barthelmes had a similar learning experience when she asked her class to write an answer to the question "Why did Mrs. Barthelmes pick *Bloomability* [Creech] for a read-aloud?" Many of her students answered by telling what they liked

FIGURE 7.1 Lizzy's informal questionnaire

Lizzy Rosso   June 11, 2001

What's your favorite thing about read aloud?

My favorite thing is when we get to a really good part and then you stop right in the middle.

What happens inside your brain during read aloud?

I try to piitchure the people or thing in my minde.

Did you learn anything about reading during read aloud that you used during your own reading?

I learnd that if a book makes you cry or laugh then it a good book.

What else did you learn during read aloud?

That you shouldn't stop in the middle of a good book. I also learnd that if a book is boring in the begining, you should keep reading because the middle will get you instred.

FIGURE 7.2 Adam's informal questionnaire

adam 6/1/01

What's your favorite thing about read aloud?

you don't have to read the book, you just listen to it.

What happens inside your brain during read aloud?

I picture what is happening in the book.

Did you learn anything about reading during read aloud that you used during your own reading?

Yes I learned how long pauses were when there were three dots, and a few words.

What else did you learn during read aloud?

I learned about authors style of writing.

about the book or what happened in the book. Only a few were able to really answer her question, showing that they understood that perhaps the big issues of being different in a new place or getting along with others might have been her reason for picking the book.

When I have modeled reading skills and strategies during read-aloud, and then provided my students with shared and guided practice in those skills and strategies during reading workshop, naturally, I expect to see the skills and strategies show up in my students' independent work. Sometimes I help this happen by focusing the responses my students are required to do with their Reading at Home assignment. For example, we

FIGURE 7.3 Tsilat's *Meet Addy* essay

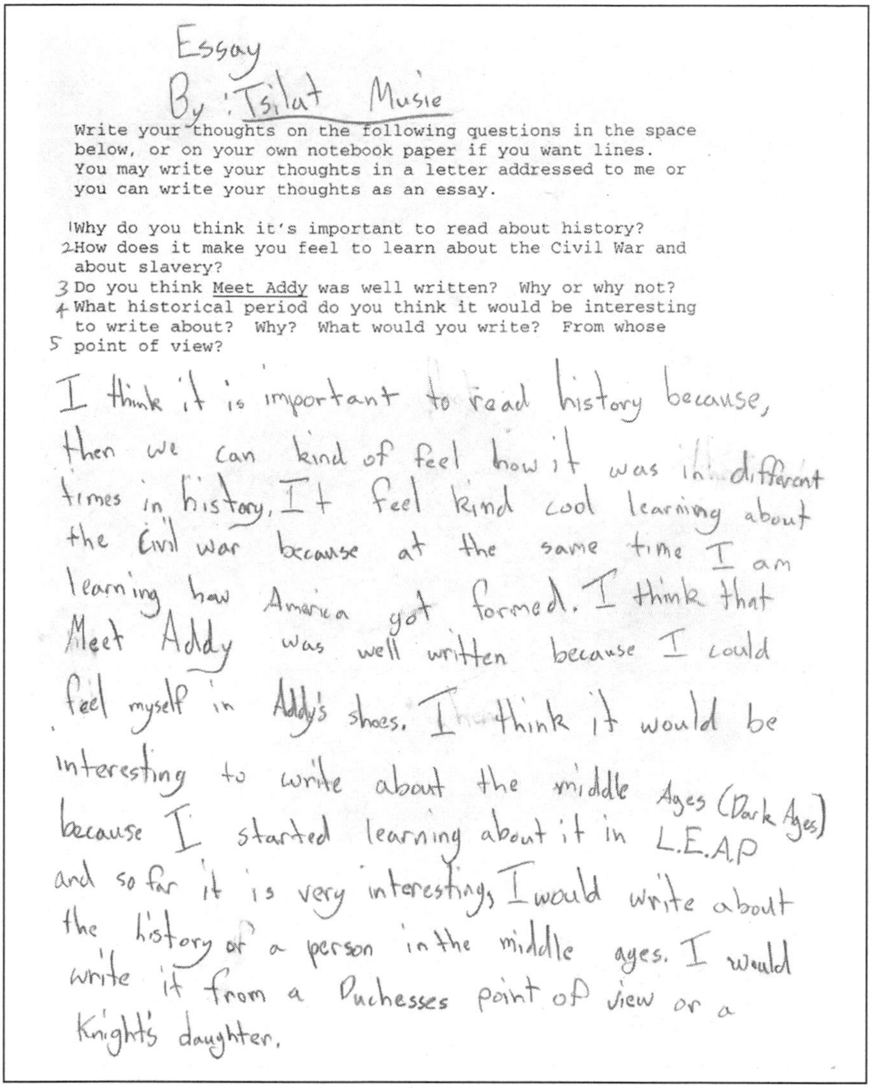

Essay
By : Tsilat Musie

Write your thoughts on the following questions in the space
below, or on your own notebook paper if you want lines.
You may write your thoughts in a letter addressed to me or
you can write your thoughts as an essay.

1 Why do you think it's important to read about history?
2 How does it make you feel to learn about the Civil War and
  about slavery?
3 Do you think <u>Meet Addy</u> was well written? Why or why not?
4 What historical period do you think it would be interesting
  to write about? Why? What would you write? From whose
5 point of view?

I think it is important to read history because,
then we can kind of feel how it was in different
times in history, It feel kind cool learning about
the Civil war because at the same time I am
learning how America got formed. I think that
Meet Addy was well written because I could
feel myself in Addy's shoes. I think it would be
interesting to write about the middle Ages (Dark Ages)
because I started learning about it in L.E.A.P
and so far it is very interesting, I would write about
the history of a person in the middle ages. I would
write it from a Duchesses point of view or a
Knight's daughter.

began our unit of study on story elements with the element of characters. We studied the characters in the read-aloud book first, then they
practiced in their independent reading in class, and finally, I asked them
to think about characters for a few more weeks in their Reading at
Home responses while in class we moved on to the story element of setting. See Appendix 2 for a selection of Reading at Home assignments

FIGURE 7.4 Tori's Reading at Home sheets

Handwritten reading log form. Top: "Tori'"

Fiction = red NonFiction = blue Poetry = yellow

DATE 4-15-02 GENRE

TITLE I was a Rat

AUTHOR Philp Pullman

#PAGES READ 7 #MINUTES READ 9:00 to 9:21 = 21 PARENT INITIALS t/e

Tell about a part of today's reading that would be a good part to illustrate. Describe how you would illustrate it. Include such details as color, use of light, point of view, placement of text, details, etc.

I would draw Roger running around with his mouth open from accidently eating pepers. I would put the text on the top of the page. It would be Roger's point of view. I would make it a little dark. I would make steam comming out of his mouth.

DATE 4-16-02 GENRE

TITLE I was a Rat

AUTHOR Philp Pullman

#PAGES READ 19 #MINUTES READ 8:50 to 9:12 = 22 PARENT INITIALS t/e

Tell about a part of today's reading that would be a good part to illustrate. Describe how you would illustrate it. Include such details as color, use of light, point of view, placement of text, details, etc.

I would draw the part when Roger had to get put in a net and got blood drawn. It would be Roger's point of view. The text would be on the left hand side. It would have a lot of light in the picture. It would have mostly dark colors.

that originated in read-aloud and in-class work before students were expected to apply the skill or strategy to their independent reading.

Sometimes all I need to do to see the evidence of the work on reading skills and strategies that started in read-aloud is be observant. When I just stand back and watch, I can see Caitlyn and Michelle using sticky notes to keep track of the main ideas in their book as they read together. I first

FIGURE 7.4 *continued*

Tori

Fiction = red   NonFiction = blue   Poetry = yellow

DATE 2-13-02   GENRE

TITLE The Battle for the Castle

AUTHOR Elizabeth Winthrop

#PAGES READ 20   #MINUTES READ 8:53 to 9:15 = 22   PARENT INITIALS ebe

Write about a connection you made to today's reading. Briefly retell the part in the book that connects, and tell about the connection in detail. Identify it as a text to self, text to text or text to world connection.

Jason won the battle against Sir Morlan! In Harry Potter Harry, Ron, and Hermione won the battle, too!

DATE 2-14-02   GENRE

TITLE The Battle for the Castle

AUTHOR Elizabeth Winthrop

#PAGES READ 18   #MINUTES READ 9:20 to 9:42 22   PARENT INITIALS ble

Write about a connection you made to today's reading. Briefly retell the part in the book that connects, and tell about the connection in detail. Identify it as a text to self, text to text or text to world connection.

Jason and William are learning how to ride a horse. I learned how to ride a horse also.

modeled that strategy in read-aloud with *Autumn Across America* (Simon). I can see Becca and her reading partner doing great vocabulary work by using the electronic spell checker as a quick dictionary as they read a challenging book together. They have learned from all of our word work during read-aloud that knowing what the unusual words mean will add to their understanding of the story. I can hear laughter—John is laughing out loud to himself during sustained silent reading. Just as we are moved to laughter, and sometimes tears, in read-aloud, so, too, is John moved when reading alone. Jessica calls me over and shows me the discoveries she's made about Count Olaf in the most recent book in The Series of Unfortunate Events. She's applying the work we did months earlier in read-aloud and reading workshop when we studied characters. Rachel wonders whether she should code the American Girls books she read for Reading at Home red for fiction or blue for nonfiction. In that one question reverberates all of the conversations we have had since *Weasel* about how all of fiction, but especially historical fiction, is a blend of fact and fiction. Go uses the class book of pictures from *Because of Winn-Dixie* to choose the part he wants for his birthday read-aloud. The pictures make concrete each child's visualization of favorite parts of the story. Go has learned that picturing the story in his mind will help him remember it.

Anecdotal

One of my two favorite tools for keeping anecdotal records is a pack of two-by-half-inch sticky notes kept handy while I'm reading. They make it easy to quickly mark the exact spot in the text where a student had a comment about the story or a question about a word. At the beginning or end of a chapter, I can make note of who made what predictions. If we are charting information from the book, it helps to keep the conversation moving if I jot the students' ideas on the sticky notes and later transfer the notes to our chart.

My other favorite tool for anecdotal record keeping is simply a spreadsheet of the class on a clipboard. During independent reading time, I can make note of the book each child is reading and any other information I might be gathering about the child's application of the skills and strategies that were taught during read-aloud.

Assessment is as unique as each person in the classroom and results in insight and infinite possibilities for learning. Assessments need not and often cannot be measured.

One day early in the year, one of my parent volunteers came in before I had had a chance to put the class's pictures from *The Van Gogh Café* by Cynthia Rylant so she could spiral-bind them. Amanda overheard our conversation and offered to put the pictures in order. I handed her the pictures and got her a copy of the book to use. Then I stood back and watched and wondered why I had been the one to put the pictures in order all along. Here was a child independently using many strategies to complete a practical task—sequencing the pictures. She went back to the text to confirm her order and to get more information. She used the chapter titles, and she skimmed the text. Her work was so amazing that when the pictures for the next book were finished, I had the whole class help me put them in order. I held the first one up and we decided whether it happened in the beginning, middle, or end. Then with each subsequent picture, we made finer and finer determinations of before and after. In the process, everyone got to see all of the pictures, so it was a form of sharing and of reflecting back on the book, as well.

Assessment, by its very nature, demands that we think about what we have noticed or heard or discovered. You don't just do an assessment, you think about it: "Discovery lies in seeing what everyone sees, but thinking what no one has thought." (Anonymous)

Recently, I have been closely examining the pictures my students make at the end of our read-alouds. I am always curious to see how they visualize the characters and the scenes, and which parts of the book they choose to draw. The class as a whole has improved the quality of work, detail, and creativity in their drawings. With each subsequent book, I look for clues as to why this has happened, such as their growth in general maturity, a deeper-than-usual connection to the book, the visual qualities in a particular book, or their practice listening to read-alouds. I wonder if the quality of the picture is linked at all to reading ability. This seems true for at least one of my students, who began the year making monotone, almost scribbled pictures. Later, at the same time he was experiencing a huge growth spurt as a reader, his pictures showed an increasing amount of story detail as well as creativity, thought, and time spent in carefully drawing and coloring his pictures.

Assessment is an essential tool for discovering strengths and weaknesses, and then formulating a plan to augment the strengths and improve the weaknesses.

I was standing at the edge of the classroom, reading aloud from *The Hour of the Olympics* (Osborne). One of the children at the table in front of me was doing something with her pencils. While I was reading, I was also watching to see if she would finish whatever she was doing, if she would realize I was watching and put her pencils away, or if I would need to quietly lean over and remind her not to fiddle with pencils during read-aloud. When I got to the bottom of the page, I realized that although my eyes had been looking at the words and my mouth had been saying what my eyes saw, I had no idea what that page of text had said. I looked up and happened to catch Tommy's eye as I said to the whole class, "Oh my gosh! I have no idea what I just read on this page! Has that ever happened to you?" I described how my attention had been on the girl with the pencils, even though my eyes had been on the book. We talked about what a reader does when he or she realizes that such an attention lapse has occurred: the reader stops and goes back to the last place that made sense, then rereads. The look of surprised recognition on Tommy's face alerted me that teaching him a strategy for monitoring his attention as he read might help improve his comprehension. The next day in reading workshop I told him about my idea. In the strategy section of his reading notebook, we created a two-column chart headed "I know what happened/I need to reread." When Tommy got to the bottom of each page in his book, he was to stop and monitor his attention and comprehension. If he knew what had happened, he would make a tally mark in the first column; if not, he would make a tally mark in the second column and reread. For several days, the number of tally marks on the reread side outnumbered the tally marks on the know-what-happened side. Then, gradually, there were fewer and fewer tallies on the reread side, until finally Tommy had internalized the strategy and stopped using the chart.

Assessment is often done by choice or has an element of choice, which results in greater empowerment.

There is no read-aloud outcome in the graded course of study, and no standard for read-aloud that is tested on the proficiency test. *Whether* I study my students' learning during read-aloud, *when* I study my students' learning during read-aloud, and *how* I study my students' learning during read-aloud are all up to me. Having choice gives me power because I can independently apply my own best professional judgment. I use my own wide range of reading to help me thoughtfully choose the books for read-aloud. When I read to my students, I base some of my teaching on my own expert knowledge of reading skills and strategies. My knowledge of the entire language arts curriculum helps me determine the skills and strategies I will teach during read-aloud. Because I view teaching as a creative art that requires disciplined spontaneity, I know when to abandon my plan, and instead to follow the students' interests and teach the skills and strategies that come up in our conversations. I am curious, I ask questions, and I design ways to discover what my students are learning during or because of read-aloud.

Choosing to assess read-aloud actually shifts the focus of assessment from my students to myself and my own teaching practices. Self-assessment happens when we watch and listen to ourselves as we teach and interact with our students. Self-assessment is informal and anecdotal, and is as unique as each teacher. Self-assessment results in insight and infinite possibilities for personal learning. When we assess our own effectiveness as a teacher, the results need not and often can not be measured. Self-assessment, by its very nature, demands that we think about what we have noticed or heard or discovered. When you choose to assess yourself, you reflect on your results. Finally, when you assess yourself and discover your particular strengths and weaknesses, you can formulate your own plan to augment your strengths and improve your weaknesses.

Choosing to assess implies a reflective stance toward teaching. Who would have believed that a whole book could be written about such a small slice of the day as read-aloud? But what I discovered, when I looked closely at read-aloud, looked closely at my teaching, and looked closely at my students' learning, was that not only are the smallest slices of our day worthy of study, but that they can also be the richest times for teaching and learning.

The "Favorites" Project

I sent out an e-mail to all the elementary and middle school teachers in my district asking those who teach (or who had taught) grades 3–6 to send me the titles and authors of their favorite read-alouds, along with a little information about why they read each favorite. I received sixty-seven responses, some within minutes of the request. Many responses began with a disclaimer like this one: "I have sooooo many favorites! Here are a few!"

The chart that follows is a peek into sixty-seven classrooms, and a hint at sixty-seven different styles of teaching. It's as much fun to browse the chart to see who agrees with your favorites as it is to glean new read-alouds. When more than one person named the same book as a favorite, I put an asterisk after the title for each subsequent time it was named. If they mentioned the topic or genre as a reason they read the book aloud, I included that in the chart. If they noted skills or other reasons for choosing the book, I included that information.

Disclaimers

This chart is intended to be only a sampling of the favorite read-alouds of an unscientifically self-selected group of teachers. It is not the be-all and end-all gospel truth of read-alouds for grades 3–6. I personally haven't read or read aloud all of the books in the chart, and I don't necessarily agree with the grade levels at which some are read. Some of the books, unfortunately, are out of print. Based on the favorites and reasons for choosing that were reported, one might conclude that in our district only a few teachers are working toward gender equity in read-aloud, and only a few are working toward racial and ethnic equity/diversity. Nonfiction is almost completely absent from the chart. But remember, this chart is a sampling, a peek at our teaching. It is not intended to be the whole picture.

And Yet . . .

Despite all its flaws, this chart is very revealing. The teachers who responded are passionate about books and about read-aloud. "Who *doesn't* read aloud to their students?" one teacher wrote. The teachers who could "pick only a few" sent lists of six to eight books. They choose read-aloud books for a complete range of reasons: because they are award winners, "quality literature," perfect for the age of their students, just right for the first book of the year or for teaching a particular reading strategy, seasonal, unique examples of author's craft, great for conversations, and just for fun.

This chart proves that read-aloud is an important time in many classrooms. Clearly, teachers use read-aloud as a teaching time, whether for the broad purpose of bringing a historical period to life, or for the narrower purpose of teaching reading skills such as visualization, prediction, point of view, vocabulary in context, inferences, and questioning. Read-aloud, as reported in this chart, spans the curriculum.

Author	Title	Grade	Subject	Topic/Genre	Reasons/Skills
Ackerman, Karen	*The Tin Heart*	4	Social Studies	History	
Alexander, Lloyd	*The Book of Three*	5			Folktale motifs, prediction, springboard for advanced readers to explore high fantasy.
Alexander, Lloyd	*The Cat Who Wished to Be a Man*	5			Humor, romance, folktale motifs, wonderful similes.
Avi	*Ereth's Birthday*	4			Character development, predictions, visualization (great language). Good follow-up to *Poppy*, which is read by third grade.
Avi	*Poppy* series ******	3–5	Library (*Poppy* with third graders)		Great humor and amazing characters you fall in love with. Poppy is a brave female character. Full of suspense. Follow the map of the adventures.
Avi	*The True Confessions of Charlotte Doyle* **	3–5			Cliffhangers, surprise ending.
Avi	*Who Stole the Wizard of Oz?*	3		Mystery	
Babbitt, Natalie	*Kneeknock Rise*	4	Science	Rocks, minerals, and land forms	Surprise ending.
Babbitt, Natalie	*Goody Hall* and *Tuck Everlasting*	5			Rich language. Great similes and metaphors.
Banks, Lynne Reid	*The Farthest Away Mountain* and *The Adventures of King Midas*	4			Predictions, learning characteristics of fantasy.

Author	Title	Grade	Subject	Topic	Comments
Banks, Lynne Reid	The Indian in the Cupboard	4			Kids love it. Character analysis.
Barnes, Peter W.	House Mouse, Senate Mouse	5	Social Studies	Government	
Bartone, Elisa	Peppe the Lamplighter *	4–5	Social Studies	History	Displays the pride and challenges of Italian immigrants.
Beatty, Patricia	Charley Skedaddle	5	Social Studies	Civil War	
Blume, Judy	Tales of a Fourth Grade Nothing **	3–4			Characters, funny.
Borntrager, Mary Christopher	Ellie	4	Social Studies	Cultural group	Amish.
Bradby, Marie	More Than Anything Else	5			A beautiful book about the gift of reading.
Brewster, Hugh	Anastasia's Album *	6	Social Studies	Russia	Lots of pictures; gruesome ending the kids love.
Bridges, Ruby	Through My Eyes **	5		Autobiography of Ruby Bridges	Fairness, bravery, civil rights. Use with The Story of Ruby Bridges by Robert Coles.
Britain, Bill	The Wish Giver *	5			Predictions, point of view, and story weaving.
Browne, Anthony	Voices in the Park *	6			Told from four different perspectives. Great for teaching about voice.
Bulla, Clyde Robert	My Friend the Monster	3		Friendship, diversity	First book of third grade.
Bunting, Eve	The Summer of Riley	5	Library		Teaches the need for compromise and acceptance.

Author	Title	Grade	Subject	Wall unit	Comment
Bunting, Eve	*The Wall*	6			Use with *Talking Walls* books.
Byars, Betsy Cromer	*After the Goat Man* or *Cracker Jackson*	4		Author study	Read aloud one of these to launch a Betsy Byars author study. Real-life problems.
Byars, Betsy Cromer	*The Moon and I*	3		Autobiography	Strong female character.
Carlson, Natalie Savage	*Family Under the Bridge*	3			Set in Paris. Different kind of family.
Charlip, Remy	*Fortunately*	6	Writing	Pattern	Students write their own book using the same pattern.
Cleary, Beverly	*Muggie Maggie*	3		Learning cursive	
Clements, Andrew	*Frindle* *****	3–5		Creating words	Fifth-grade character, great relationship with teacher at the end.
Collier, James Lincoln and Christopher Collier	*The Clock*	4		Historical fiction	
Collier, James Lincoln and Christopher Collier	*My Brother Sam Is Dead*	5	Social Studies	Revolutionary War	
Conrad, Pam	*My Daniel*	5			Slow starting, but worth it. Good for studying flashbacks.
Conrad, Pam	*Pedro's Journal*	5	Social Studies	Explorers	Point of view of the cabin boy.
Coville, Bruce	*Jeremy Thatcher, Dragon Hatcher*	5		Science fiction, fantasy	

Author	Title	Grade	Subject	Topic	Notes
Creech, Sharon	Bloomability	5			Tolerance, dealing with change.
Creech, Sharon	Love That Dog	5			Written in free-verse poetry as a journal of a boy who comes to realize he can write poetry. Quick read.
Creech, Sharon	Pleasing the Ghost	4			Vocabulary in context, inferences.
Creech, Sharon	Walk Two Moons *	5			Author's craft, questioning and predicting.
Cronin, Doreen	Click, Clack, Moo: Cows That Type*	6		Fun story illustrates issues related to labor, strikes, and negotiation.	Great for teaching problem/solution. Caldecott Honor Book.
Curtis, Christopher Paul	The Watsons Go to Birmingham—1963 **	3–5		Civil rights	Serious title, funny scenes—great contrast teaches kids not to judge a book by the cover. Family relationships.
Dahl, Roald	The BFG	3–4			Kids love it.
Dahl, Roald	Boy	5		Autobiography	Tells the seeds of his book ideas.
Dahl, Roald	Charlie and the Chocolate Factory	3	Health	Nutrition/chocolate unit	
Dahl, Roald	George's Marvelous Medicine	3		Germs	
Dahl, Roald	James and the Giant Peach	3–4			Adventure, fantasy.
Dahl, Roald	The Magic Finger	3			Predictions.
Dahl, Roald	Matilda*	3–4			Kids love it!

Author	Title	Grade	Subject	Topic	Notes
Davidson, Margaret	*I Have a Dream*	3		Biography, Martin Luther King Jr.	
DeClements, Barthe	*The Fourth Grade Wizards*	4			Character development and motivation.
DeFelice, Cynthia	*Weasel* **	4	Social Studies	Ohio history	
De Saint Phalle, Niki	*AIDS: You Can't Catch It Holding Hands*	8	Health		Good, quick, sensitive summary of answers to common questions about AIDS.
DiCamillo, Kate	*Because of Winn-Dixie* *	4–5			What a powerful story! For once the dog doesn't die!
Dorris, Michael	*Morning Girl*	5–6	Social Studies	Explorers—Columbus	Told from the point of view of a Native child.
Duffey, Betsy	*How to Be Cool in the Third Grade*	3			Ice breaker at the beginning of the year.
Duffey, Betsy	*The Gadget War*	3–4	Science	Simple machines	
Edwards, Julie Andrews	*The Last of the Really Great Whangdoodles*	3–4			Importance of creativity and using your imagination.
Estes, Eleanor	*The Hundred Dresses*	4		Friendship	
Fields, Terri	*The Day Fifth Grade Disappeared*	5		First or last book of the year.	
Fletcher, Ralph	*Fig Pudding* ****	3–4			Characterization. Great for conversations. Importance of family and caring for others.

Author	Title	Grade	Subject	Topic	Notes
Fletcher, Ralph	Twilight Comes Twice	6			Great to use with visualizing.
Forbes, Esther	Johnny Tremain	5	Social Studies	U.S. history, historical fiction, Revolutionary War	Compare and contrast then and now.
Gardiner, John Reynolds	Stone Fox	3			
George, Jean Craighead	Animals Who Have Won Our Hearts	3–5		Animals in history	Great nonfiction read-aloud. Each chapter is like a short story.
George, Jean Craighead	Look to the North: A Wolf Pup Diary	6		Story about the birth and growth of wolf pups.	Great for teaching about sequence.
Giff, Patricia Reilly	Lilly's Crossing	5		Wars—WWII	Friendships on the home front.
Good, Merle	Reuben and the Blizzard *	6			Great for making predictions.
Goodman, Joan Elizabeth	Hope's Crossing	5	Social Studies	Revolutionary War	
Greenwald, Sheila	Write On, Rosy	3			Writing process.
Haddix, Margaret Peterson	Among the Hidden	4		Science fiction	Set in the future, told by a third child in a society that allows only two children per family.
Haddix, Margaret Peterson	Running Out of Time	5	Social Studies	Colonization	

Hall, Donald	The Ox-Cart Man	4	Social Studies	Economics	
Haskins, James	Get on Board	5		Abolitionists	Great time line of abolitionists.
Heide, Florence Parry and Judith Heide Gilliland	The Day of Ahmed's Secret	6			Great for questioning strategies.
Heller, Ruth	A Cache of Jewels	3–5	Language Arts	Parts of speech	Nouns.
Heller, Ruth	Fantastic! Wow! and Unreal!	3–5	Language Arts	Parts of speech	Interjections and conjunctions.
Heller, Ruth	Kites Sail High	3–5	Language Arts	Parts of speech	Verbs.
Heller, Ruth	Many Luscious Lollipops	3–5	Language Arts	Parts of speech	Adjectives.
Heller, Ruth	Mine, All Mine	3–5	Language Arts	Parts of speech	Pronouns.
Heller, Ruth	Up, Up and Away	3–5	Language Arts	Parts of speech	Adverbs.
Henkes, Kevin	Chrysanthemum	3–5			Text-to-self connections, questioning, thinking aloud.
Henkes, Kevin	Lilly's Purple Plastic Purse **	6			Great for teaching literary elements and characterization.
Hesse, Karen	Letters from Rifka *	3–4	Social Studies	Immigration	Strong female character.
Hinton, S. E.	The Outsiders	6			Audio book. Compare book and movie.
Hobbs, Will	Far North	5			High interest, high adventure.
Hopkins, Lee Bennett, compiler	Hand in Hand: An American History Through Poetry	6		Poetry	Organized around milestones in U.S. history.
Hopkinson, Deborah	Sweet Clara and the Freedom Quilt	5			African slave fantasy.

Howe, James	I Wish I Were a Butterfly	3–5	Self-esteem	
Howe, James and Deborah Howe	Bunnicula	3	Halloween	
Hurwitz, Johanna	The Just Desserts Club	5	Library	Fun food extensions possible.
Jacques, Brian	Mossflower and Redwall	5		Colorful language, brilliant descriptions of characters and settings.
Jones, Charlotte Foltz	Mistakes that Worked *	4–6		Shows it's okay to make mistakes as long as we learn from them. Sometimes things work out, just not as we intended.
Jones, Ron	The Acorn People	6	Self-awareness, self-esteem	
Jukes, Mavis	Blackberries in the Dark	5	Family traditions, loss	
Juster, Norton	The Phantom Tollbooth	5		Skilled listeners with previous experience understanding puns required.
Karr, Kathleen	The Great Turkey Walk	5		The author takes a little-known historical fact and creates characters and a situation that students can easily imagine.
Katz, William Loren	Black Women of the Old West	5		Contributions of black women in the development of the West. Photographs.
Knight, Margy Burns	Talking Walls and Talking Walls: The Stories Continue	6	Walls unit	Map and detailed information about each wall at the end.

Author	Title	Grade	Subject	Topic	Notes
Konigsburg, E. L.	The View from Saturday	5			Author's craft in weaving the plot. Great for discussions of how kids treat each other.
Lasky, Kathryn	A Journey to the New World	5	Social Studies	Pilgrims	
Lewis, C. S.	The Lion, The Witch and the Wardrobe*	4–5			Foreshadowing, symbolism, descriptive language, great fantasy.
Lyon, George Ella	Who Came Down That Road?	4	Social Studies	History	
MacLachlan, Patricia	Baby *	3–5			So much to discover about themes and author's craft.
MacLachlan, Patricia	Sarah, Plain and Tall	3			Beautiful language.
Martin, Rafe	The Rough-Face Girl	5	Library	Cinderella variant	
Mayer, Marianna	Baba Yaga and Vasilisa the Brave	5	Library	Halloween	
Mayle, Peter	"What's Happening to Me?"	8	Health		Introduction to human sexuality topics.
McCully, Emily Arnold	Ballot Box Battle	4	Library	Women's History Month	Fictional biography.
McKissack, Pat	Christmas in the Big House, Christmas in the Quarters	5			Contrasts the planters' Christmas celebration with the slaves'. Five-star illustrations.
Merrill, Jean	The Toothpaste Millionaire ****	4–5	Social Studies	Economics	Teaches factors of production. The entrepreneur is a boy.

Author	Title	Grade	Genre/Subject	Notes
Mitchell, Barbara	A Pocketful of Goobers	3	Biography. George Washington Carver	Action and adventure.
Morey, Walt	Gentle Ben	3		Substance abuse and a work dog.
Morey, Walt	Hero	5	Mystery	
Mowat, Farley	Owls in the Family	3		Vocabulary (from Canada) in context, funny.
Munsch, Robert N.	Love You Forever	6		Classroom bonding.
Myers, Walter Dean	Amistad: A Long Road to Freedom	5	Slavery	Excellent account of life on a "slave ship."
Naylor, Phyllis Reynolds	The Boys Start the War	3–5		Kids their age, just for fun.
Naylor, Phyllis Reynolds	Shiloh trilogy ***	3–4	Realistic fiction	Characters, cliffhangers, predictions, inferences.
Nelson, Ray, Douglas Kelly, and Michelle Roehm	Connie and Bonnie's Birthday Blastoff	7	Science	Kick off a unit of study.
Nelson, Ray, and Doug Kelly	Seven Seas of Billy's Bathtub	7	Science	Kick off a unit of study.
Nelson, Ray, Doug Kelly, Ben Adams, and Julie Mohr	The Munchy Crunchy Bug Book	7	Science	Kick off a unit of study.

Author	Title				
Neuschwander, Cindy	Sir Cumference series	6	Math	Area and geometry	
Newmann, Steven M.	Worldwalk	6	Social Studies	World cultures	
Park, Barbara	The Kid in the Red Jacket	5			New kid on the block issues.
Park, Barbara	Skinnybones	3			Perfect humor for third graders.
Paterson, Katherine	Bridge to Terabithia	5			Relationships, handling death.
Paulsen, Gary	Hatchet ***	4			Many life lessons: learning to help yourself, positive attitude, courage, and survival. Motivates students (often boys who are reluctant readers) to read all of the sequels.
Paulsen, Gary	Soldier's Heart	5	Social Studies	Civil War	
Paulsen, Gary	The Transall Saga	5			Science fiction.
Paulsen, Gary	Woodsong	6		Iditarod	Audio book, read by Gary Paulsen.
Peck, Richard	A Long Way from Chicago *	3–5		Great Depression	Funny.
Philbrick, Rodman	Freak the Mighty *	5–6			Underdog characters. Unique friendship. The movie is just as good as the book.
Pinkwater, Daniel Manus	The Hoboken Chicken Emergency	3–4		Thanksgiving	Funny and seasonal.
Polacco, Patricia	Pink and Say ****	5–6	Social Studies	Civil War	Friendship that crosses the color lines.

Author	Title	Grade	Subject	Theme	Notes
Polacco, Patricia	Thank You, Mr. Falker	3–5		Beginning of the year	We all have strengths and weaknesses. Text-to-self connections.
Precek, Katharine Wilson	The Keepsake Chest	4	Social Studies	Ohio history	
Raskin, Ellen	The Westing Game	5		Mystery	
Rawls, Wilson	Summer of the Monkeys ****	3–4		Determination	Cause and effect, similes, metaphors, and personification. Great animal story. New to most students.
Rawls, Wilson	Where the Red Fern Grows **	3–4		Determination	Great animal story. Keep the tissue box close at hand.
Ray, Mary Lyn	Shaker Boy	4	Social Studies	Cultural group	Shaker.
Robinson, Barbara	The Best Christmas Pageant Ever	3–4		Christmas	Funny and seasonal.
Robinson, Barbara	Trace Through the Forest	4	Social Studies	Ohio history	Great cliffhangers.
Rowling, J. K.	Harry Potter and the Sorcerer's Stone	4			Even reluctant readers love this book, and it empowers them to read along and discuss it with the class.
Rylant, Cynthia	Every Living Thing	3			Short stories, prediction, inferences.
Rylant, Cynthia	Gooseberry Park	3–4		Friendship	Funny.
Rylant, Cynthia	The Islander *	3–4			Questioning. Story of a boy and his grandfather.
Rylant, Cynthia	The Relatives Came	6			Great for making connections. Caldecott Honor Book.

Author	Title	Grade			Notes
Rylant, Cynthia	The Van Gogh Café **	3–5		Imaginative and magical	Inferences, questioning, predicting.
Sachar, Louis	Holes ****	3–5			Survival story. Author's craft. Flashbacks and complex plot.
Sachar, Louis	There's a Boy in the Girls' Bathroom *	5		First book of the year	Funny. Main character is that "unique" kid that we've all had at one time or another.
San Souci, Robert D.	Brave Margaret	4	Library	St. Patrick's Day	Irish folktale.
Sanders, Scott Russell	The Floating House	4	Social Studies	History	
Sanders, Scott Russell	Warm as Wool	4	Social Studies	History	
Say, Allen	Grandfather's Journey	6			Story of the author's life in Japan and the U.S. Great for teaching compare/contrast.
Scieszka, Jon	Baloney (Henry P.) *	4–6			Foreign words are sprinkled throughout the story. Great to use when teaching about using context clues to figure out unfamiliar words.
Scieszka, Jon	Squids Will Be Squids	6		Updated fables with fun illustrations.	Great to use to teach about morals and/or themes.
Scieszka, Jon	Summer Reading Is Killing Me!	5			Literary allusions to children's stories at all different reading levels.

Author	Title		Subject	Topic	Point of view.
Scieszka, Jon	The True Story of the Three Little Pigs	5			Point of view.
Selden, George	The Cricket in Times Square	3–4		Animal characters	Award winner. Classic literature.
Selden, George	Tucker's Countryside	3–4		Animal characters, Earth Day	Award winner. Classic literature.
Shyer, Marlene Fanta	Welcome Home, Jellybean	4	Health	Disabilities	
Skurzynski, Gloria	Lost in the Devil's Desert	3	Social Studies, Science	World regions and land forms	Great survival adventure book.
Smith, Robert Kimmel	The War With Grandpa *	3–5			Compromise and family values.
Snicket, Lemony	The Bad Beginning from A Series of Unfortunate Events	5	Library		Unexpected events keep the listeners guessing.
Speare, Elizabeth George	The Sign of the Beaver *	4	Social Studies	Pioneers	
St. George, Judith	So You Want to Be President?	5	Social Studies	Presidents	
Stevens, Janet	And the Dish Ran Away With the Spoon *	3–5			Humor, puns, literary allusions to Mother Goose rhymes and characters.
Stewart, Sarah	The Gardener	6		Depression era	Written in letter format. Great for sequencing strategies.
Strauss, Linda Leopold	A Fairy Called Hilary	3	Library		Promotes discussions about everyday magic, "what ifs," and the importance of friendship.

Author	Title	Grade	Subject	Notes
Taylor, Mildred	*The Friendship* and *The Gold Cadillac* *	3–6	Relationships between blacks and whites	Good to read before Martin Luther King Day or during Black History Month.
Taylor, Mildred	*Roll of Thunder, Hear My Cry*	4		Issues that are extremely important for Northerners to understand. Written from the heart by an author who lived it.
Taylor, Theodore	*The Cay* **	5		Survival, friendship, diversity, prejudice.
Trent, John, Cindy Trent, Gary Smalley, and Norma Smalley	*The Treasure Tree* *	3–5	Cooperation, understanding strengths and weaknesses	First book at the beginning of the year.
Van Allsburg, Chris	*Just a Dream*	6	Science Ecology, pollution	Prompts students to explore their views of the future.
Van Allsburg, Chris	*The Mysteries of Harris Burdick*	6	Writing	Students select a picture and title, then write their own story.
Van Allsburg, Chris	*The Stranger*	6	Writing	Students write character sketches of their own Jack Frost.
Van Allsburg, Chris	*The Widow's Broom*	6	Halloween	Just for fun.
Van Draanen, Wendelin	*Sammy Keyes* series	3–5	Mystery	
Van Leevwen, Jean	*The Great Christmas Kidnapping Caper* *	3–5	Mystery, holiday	Predictions, visualizing, modeling dialogue, intonation, and sheer fun during the holiday season. Doesn't say whether or not Santa is real, so it is fun for those who aren't sure yet.

		4	Library		Fun.
Vande Velde, Vivian	Smart Dog				
Vigna, Judith	I Wish Daddy Didn't Drink So Much	8	Health		Introduction to dysfunctional families and alcoholism.
Vigna, Judith	My Big Sister Takes Drugs	7	Health		Insightful look at how taking drugs can affect your entire family.
Wallace, Bill	Watchdog and the Coyotes **	3		Friendship and courage	Making inferences.
Walsh, Jill Paton	The Green Book *	3–5		Science fiction	Good for a pioneer unit—how life would be different for us if we had to move to another planet.
Wardlaw, Lee	101 Ways to Bug Your Parents	3–4			Start off the year on a light note.
White, E. B.	Charlotte's Web	3			Visualization.
White, E. B.	Stuart Little	3			Children love to imagine mouse character's adventures. Nothing like the movie.
White, E. B.	Trumpet of the Swan	4			Great characters, good example of journaling and questioning.
Wick, Walter	A Drop of Water	6		Nonfiction	Great for practice coding text.
Wilder, Laura Ingalls	Little House in the Big Woods	3–4		Historical fiction	
Willard, Nancy	The High Rise Glorious Skittle Skat Roarious Sky Pie Angel Food Cake	3			Excellent language, dialogue, anticipation, personal connections, magic, and story layering.

Willis, Patricia	*Danger Along the Ohio* **	4	Social Studies	Ohio history	
Wisniewski, David	*Tough Cookie*	5			Play on words.
Wright, Betty Ren	*The Ghost Comes Calling*	3	Library		Expressions are a little dated but third graders love this ghost story.
Yolen, Jane	*Encounter* ***	5–6	Social Studies	Explorers—Columbus	Told from the point of view of a Native child.

Reading at Home

I expect my students to read for twenty minutes or more each night. I have experimented with different ways for them to report on their reading, but nothing has worked as well as the current Reading at Home sheets. I run the sheets back-to-back so that there are four sections, one each for their reading on Monday–Thursday nights. The RAH sheets are turned in on Fridays in the students' RAH folders.

In the header is a reminder of the colors we use to code the genres of the books. Coloring in the genre boxes is a visual reminder that I want my students to read a variety of genres (Taberski 2000).

The topics for the bit of writing I ask my students to do each night after reading come directly from the lessons I have taught in class: modeled in the read-aloud, and shared, guided, and practiced in reading workshop.

Fiction = red   Nonfiction = blue   Poetry = yellow   Genre

Date _____

Title _____

Author _____

Pages Read _____   # Minutes Read _____ to _____   Guardian's Initials _____

Character's name:

What today's reading told me about this character:

Fiction = red   Nonfiction = blue   Poetry = yellow   Genre

Date _____

Title _____

Author _____

Pages Read _____   # Minutes Read _____ to _____   Guardian's Initials _____

Character's name:

What today's reading told me about this character:

Fiction = red   Nonfiction = blue   Poetry = yellow   Genre

Date _____

Title _____

Author _____

Pages Read _____   # Minutes Read _____ to _____   Guardian's Initials _____

What my character did:

What that tells me about my character:

Fiction = red   Nonfiction = blue   Poetry = yellow   Genre

Date _____

Title _____

Author _____

Pages Read _____   # Minutes Read _____ to _____   Guardian's Initials _____

What my character did:

What that tells me about my character:

Fiction = red   Nonfiction = blue   Poetry = yellow   Genre [ ]

Date _____

Title _____

Author _____

Pages Read _____   # Minutes Read _____ to _____   Guardian's Initials _____

Words to describe a character in my book:

My analysis of that character:

Fiction = red   Nonfiction = blue   Poetry = yellow   Genre [ ]

Date _____

Title _____

Author _____

Pages Read _____   # Minutes Read _____ to _____   Guardian's Initials _____

Words to describe a character in my book:

My analysis of that character:

Fiction = red   Nonfiction = blue   Poetry = yellow   Genre ☐

Date _____

Title _____

Author _____

Pages Read _____   # Minutes Read _____ to _____   Guardian's Initials _____

Describe the setting in today's reading:

Tell about my scene changes:

Fiction = red   Nonfiction = blue   Poetry = yellow   Genre ☐

Date _____

Title _____

Author _____

Pages Read _____   # Minutes Read _____ to _____   Guardian's Initials _____

Describe the setting in today's reading:

Tell about my scene changes:

Fiction = red   Nonfiction = blue   Poetry = yellow   Genre

Date _____

Title _____

Author _____

\# Pages Read _____   \# Minutes Read _____ to _____   Guardian's Initials _____

Words to describe a setting in my book:

My analysis of the author's use of or choice of that setting:

Fiction = red   Nonfiction = blue   Poetry = yellow   Genre

Date _____

Title _____

Author _____

\# Pages Read _____   \# Minutes Read _____ to _____   Guardian's Initials _____

Words to describe a setting in my book:

My analysis of the author's use of or choice of that setting:

Fiction = red   Nonfiction = blue   Poetry = yellow   Genre

Date _____

Title _____

Author _____

Pages Read _____   # Minutes Read _____ to _____   Guardian's Initials _____

Beginning ⟶ **Middle** ⟶ **End**

Fiction = red   Nonfiction = blue   Poetry = yellow   Genre

Date _____

Title _____

Author _____

Pages Read _____   # Minutes Read _____ to _____   Guardian's Initials _____

Beginning ⟶ **Middle** ⟶ **End**

Fiction = red   Nonfiction = blue   Poetry = yellow   Genre

Date _____

Title _____

Author _____

Pages Read _____   # Minutes Read _____ to _____   Guardian's Initials _____

Write a short summary of tonight's reading. Respond to what you read.

Fiction = red   Nonfiction = blue   Poetry = yellow   Genre

Date _____

Title _____

Author _____

Pages Read _____   # Minutes Read _____ to _____   Guardian's Initials _____

Write a short summary of tonight's reading. Respond to what you read.

Fiction = red   Nonfiction = blue   Poetry = yellow   Genre

Date _____

Title _____

Author _____

Pages Read _____   # Minutes Read _____ to _____   Guardian's Initials _____

Your Choice: Write about the characters, the setting, or retell the plot.

Fiction = red   Nonfiction = blue   Poetry = yellow   Genre

Date _____

Title _____

Author _____

Pages Read _____   # Minutes Read _____ to _____   Guardian's Initials _____

Your Choice: Write about the characters, the setting, or retell the plot.

Fiction = red   Nonfiction = blue   Poetry = yellow   Genre

Date _____

Title _____

Author _____

Pages Read _____   # Minutes Read _____ to _____   Guardian's Initials _____

The topic of my nonfiction book (who or what):

The setting (where and/or when) of my nonfiction book:

A few cool facts I learned in tonight's nonfiction reading:

Fiction = red   Nonfiction = blue   Poetry = yellow   Genre

Date _____

Title _____

Author _____

Pages Read _____   # Minutes Read _____ to _____   Guardian's Initials _____

The topic of my nonfiction book (who or what):

The setting (where and/or when) of my nonfiction book:

A few cool facts I learned in tonight's nonfiction reading:

Fiction = red   Nonfiction = blue   Poetry = yellow   Genre

Date _____

Title _____

Author _____

Pages Read _____   # Minutes Read _____ to _____   Guardian's Initials _____

A few cool facts I learned in tonight's nonfiction reading, and my opinion of those facts:

Fact:

Opinion:

Fact:

Opinion:

Fact:

Opinion:

Fiction = red   Nonfiction = blue   Poetry = yellow   Genre

Date _____

Title _____

Author _____

Pages Read _____   # Minutes Read _____ to _____   Guardian's Initials _____

A few cool facts I learned in tonight's nonfiction reading, and my opinion of those facts:

Fact:

Opinion:

Fact:

Opinion:

Fact:

Opinion:

Reconsidering Read-Aloud by Mary Lee Hahn. Copyright © 2002. Stenhouse Publishers.

Fiction = red   Nonfiction = blue   Poetry = yellow   Genre

Date _____

Title _____

Author _____

Pages Read _____   # Minutes Read _____ to _____   Guardian's Initials _____

Write about a connection you made to today's reading. Briefly retell the part in the book that connects, and tell about the connection in detail. Identify it as a text-to-self, text-to-text, or text-to-world connection.

Fiction = red   Nonfiction = blue   Poetry = yellow   Genre

Date _____

Title _____

Author _____

Pages Read _____   # Minutes Read _____ to _____   Guardian's Initials _____

Write about a connection you made to today's reading. Briefly retell the part in the book that connects, and tell about the connection in detail. Identify it as a text-to-self, text-to-text, or text-to-world connection.

Fiction = red   Nonfiction = blue   Poetry = yellow   Genre

Date _____

Title _____

Author _____

Pages Read _____   # Minutes Read _____ to _____   Guardian's Initials _____

Write some of the questions that occurred to you as you read. Were they answered as you read on? If not, what do you predict the answer might be?

Fiction = red   Nonfiction = blue   Poetry = yellow   Genre

Date _____

Title _____

Author _____

Pages Read _____   # Minutes Read _____ to _____   Guardian's Initials _____

Write some of the questions that occurred to you as you read. Were they answered as you read on? If not, what do you predict the answer might be?

Fiction = red   Nonfiction = blue   Poetry = yellow   Genre

Date _____

Title _____

Author _____

Pages Read _____   # Minutes Read _____ to _____   Guardian's Initials _____

What part in tonight's reading did you mark with a sticky note to talk about with your partner? Why did you mark that part?

Fiction = red   Nonfiction = blue   Poetry = yellow   Genre

Date _____

Title _____

Author _____

Pages Read _____   # Minutes Read _____ to _____   Guardian's Initials _____

What part in tonight's reading did you mark with a sticky note to talk about with your partner? Why did you mark that part?

Fiction = red   Nonfiction = blue   Poetry = yellow   Genre [ ]

Date _____

Title _____

Author _____

Pages Read _____   # Minutes Read _____ to _____   Guardian's Initials _____

Write a note to the author of your book, telling her/him what she/he did well in her/his writing, or what she/he could work on to make better.

Fiction = red   Nonfiction = blue   Poetry = yellow   Genre [ ]

Date _____

Title _____

Author _____

Pages Read _____   # Minutes Read _____ to _____   Guardian's Initials _____

Write a note to the author of your book, telling her/him what she/he did well in her/his writing, or what she/he could work on to make better.

Reconsidering Read-Aloud by Mary Lee Hahn. Copyright © 2002. Stenhouse Publishers.

Fiction = red   Nonfiction = blue   Poetry = yellow   Genre [ ]

Date _____

Title _____

Author _____

Pages Read _____   # Minutes Read _____ to _____   Guardian's Initials _____

Tell about a part in today's reading that would be a good part to illustrate. Describe how you would illustrate it. Include such details as color, use of light, point of view, placement of text, details, etc.

Fiction = red   Nonfiction = blue   Poetry = yellow   Genre [ ]

Date _____

Title _____

Author _____

Pages Read _____   # Minutes Read _____ to _____   Guardian's Initials _____

Tell about a part in today's reading that would be a good part to illustrate. Describe how you would illustrate it. Include such details as color, use of light, point of view, placement of text, details, etc.

Read-Aloud as a Teaching Time

Some people think read-aloud should never, under any circumstances, be used as a teaching time. For them, read-aloud is a "sacred" time consisting only of the pure enjoyment of literature. If I met such a person, I think we would disagree more about what constitutes teaching than what read-aloud should be like. If they have chosen a book to read to their students that they love, and that they hope their students will love, then I would say that at the very minimum, they are teaching the love and appreciation of great literature. If they ever stop to explain a vocabulary word, discuss a confusing part, or ask their students what they think of the book, again, I would say they are teaching during read-aloud.

A "read-aloud purist" might argue that they are protecting their students' love of literature by keeping read-aloud a time of pure enjoyment. If I heard that, I would wonder first if that teacher was a reader him- or herself. Next, I would wonder what kind of teacher views teaching as an act that destroys enjoyment rather than enhances it. By protecting read-aloud from teaching, are they protecting their students, or trying to make their own job easier? Are things that are fun only those that are devoid of rigorous work, reflective practice, and the creative act of disciplined spontaneity?

Most teachers need only to closely examine their read-aloud to find all the teaching that they are already doing, or the teachable moments that they can use. The chart that follows identifies attitude shifts that occur when read-aloud is recognized as a teaching time.

Less of This

Read aloud a book your best friend has recommended without previewing it first.

More of This

Read every book that is a candidate for read-aloud all the way through before reading it aloud, no matter who recommends it to you. At the very least it will give you a better idea of what to teach, and when, but it will also alert you to the times in the book when you might need to have the tissue box handy, or language you might want to skip or modify. And face it—you might not like the book!

Read aloud only fiction.

In between the fiction chapter books you read aloud (or sometimes during, if it fits or if you need a one-day break), read short nonfiction, magazine and newspaper articles, and your favorite picture books.

Read aloud the same books every year.

Read widely and constantly. Always be on the lookout for a book, article, or poem that would be perfect for read-aloud. Browse print and electronic resources that review children's books. Take children's literature courses. Stay fresh; try new things. If you are bored with your read-aloud, you can guarantee your students will be.

Choose books for read-aloud that are well above the reading level of most of your students. Read them books they couldn't read on their own.

Validate the reading of every child in your class by reading aloud books from the lowest as well as the highest levels of your readers. Some of my students' deepest responses are sometimes to the simplest texts.

Stay seated while reading aloud.

Stand during read-aloud so that your voice better projects throughout the room. If you move around the room during read-aloud, you can monitor attentiveness and deal with a student's minor lapse of attention in a private and unobtrusive way.

Have students do round-robin reading and call it read-aloud.

During read-aloud, the most able reader in the room—the teacher—reads aloud to students. Because the teacher does the work of decoding the text and reading it fluently with expression, the students are better able to practice strategies and habits of mind that are critical for comprehension, such as visualizing the text as it is read, making predictions and inferences, questioning, making connections, determining importance, and synthesizing information (Harvey and Goudvis 2000).

Do read-aloud when you get the chance, or to reward your students for good behavior.

Read aloud for 20–30 minutes a day (including pre- and post-reading discussions). When you get the chance, and when your students are ready, read aloud for as long as an hour or more. Read aloud several times during the day from different genres of texts so that students have the experience of listening to more than just fiction chapter books. Make read-aloud an integral part of your reading instruction, not a carrot for your discipline plan.

Consider read-aloud a minor component of language arts.

Read-aloud is the heart of reading instruction and informs and influences every aspect of language arts. Read-aloud is where the skills and strategies of a fluent reader are modeled and students are able, in a risk-free environment, to practice those skills and strategies.

Write lesson plans for read-aloud.

Teach spontaneously during read-aloud. As a fluent and metacognitive reader, you will find more literacy lessons than you ever could or should teach in every book you read aloud. Because you know your students well, and you know your goals for reading and language arts, you will be able to decide on a moment-to-moment and page-by-page basis as you read aloud whether to focus on making predictions, analyzing characters, determining the meaning of vocabulary in context, and so on. Also be ready and willing to let your teaching follow your students' interests, developmental stages, and needs as readers.

Bibliography

Ackerman, Diane. 2001. *Cultivating Delight*. New York: HarperCollins.

Ada, Alma Flor. 1994. *Dear Peter Rabbit*. New York: Atheneum.

———. 1998. *Yours Truly, Goldilocks*. New York: Atheneum.

———. 2001. *With Love, Little Red Hen*. New York: Atheneum.

Armstrong, Lance. 2001. *It's Not About the Bike: My Journey Back to Life*. New York: Berkley Books.

Avi. 2000. *The True Confessions of Charlotte Doyle*. St. Paul, MN: EMC/Paradigm.

Bauer, Marion Dane. 1986. *On My Honor*. Boston: G. K. Hall.

Baylor, Byrd. 1994. *The Table Where the Rich People Sit*. New York: Scribner's.

Blume, Judy. 1972. *Tales of a Fourth Grade Nothing*. New York: Dutton.

Bosveld, Jane. 1997. *While a Tree Was Growing*. New York: American Museum of Natural History/Workman.

Bridges, Ruby. 1999. *Through My Eyes*. New York: Scholastic.

Bunting, Eve. 1998. *So Far from the Sea*. New York: Clarion Books.

Burnett, Francis Hodgson. 1915. *The Secret Garden*. New York: Grosset & Dunlap.

Byars, Betsy Cromer. 1991. *The Moon and I*. New York: J. Messner.

Calkins, Lucy. 2001. *The Art of Teaching Reading*. New York: Addison-Wesley.

Chevalier, Tracy. 1999. *Girl with a Pearl Earring*. London: HarperCollins.

Clements, Andrew. 1996. *Frindle*. New York: Simon & Schuster Books for Young Readers.

Coles, Robert. 1995. *The Story of Ruby Bridges*. New York: Scholastic.

Collier, James Lincoln, and Christopher Collier. 1992. *The Clock*. New York: Delacorte Press.

Cosby, Bill. Little Bill Books for Beginning Readers Series. New York: Scholastic.

Creech, Sharon. 1994. *Walk Two Moons*. New York: HarperCollins Children's Books.

———. 1998. *Bloomability*. New York: HarperCollins.

Curtis, Christopher Paul. 1995. *The Watsons Go to Birmingham—1963*. New York: Delacorte Press.

———. 1999. *Bud, Not Buddy*. New York: Delacorte Press.

Dahl, Roald. 1961. *James and the Giant Peach*. New York: Knopf.

DeFelice, Cynthia. 1990. *Weasel*. New York: Avon Books.

DiCamillo, Kate. 2000. *Because of Winn-Dixie*. Cambridge, MA: Candlewick Press.

Dorris, Michael. 1992. *Morning Girl*. New York: Hyperion Books for Children.

Fletcher, Ralph. 1995. *Fig Pudding*. New York: Bantam Doubleday Dell Books for Young Readers.

———. 2001. *Uncle Daddy*. New York: Henry Holt.

Fountas, Irene C., and Gay Su Pinnell. 2001. *Guiding Readers and Writers Grades 3–6: Teaching Comprehension, Genre, and Content Literacy*. Portsmouth, NH: Heinemann.

Fox, Mem. 2001. *Reading Magic: Why Reading Aloud to Our Children Will Change Their Lives Forever*. New York: Harcourt.

Fuschuber, Annegert. 1998. *Mouse Tale/Giant Story*. Minneapolis: Carolrhoda Books.

George, Jean Craighead. 1996. *The Tarantula in My Purse: And 172 Other Wild Pets*. New York: HarperCollins.

Ghazi, Suhaib Hamid. 1996. *Ramadan*. New York: Holiday House.

Gipson, Fred. 1956. *Old Yeller*. New York: Harper.

Harvey, Stephanie, and Anne Goudvis. 2000. *Strategies That Work: Teaching Comprehension to Enhance Understanding*. Portland, ME: Stenhouse.

Hesse, Karen. 1998. *Just Juice*. New York: Scholastic.

Hooks, William. 1989. *The Three Little Pigs and the Fox*. New York: Macmillan.

Huck, Charlotte S., Susan Hepler, and Janet Hickman. 1987. *Children's Literature in the Elementary School*. New York: Holt, Rinehart, and Winston.

Jacques, Brian. 1986. *Redwall*. New York: Philomel Books.

Keene, Ellin Oliver, and Susan Zimmerman. 1997. *Mosaic of Thought*. Portsmouth, NH: Heinemann.

Lave, Jean, and Etienne Wenger. 1991. *Situated Learning: Legitimate Peripheral Participation*. Cambridge: Cambridge University Press.

Lowry, Lois. 1993. *The Giver*. Boston: Houghton Mifflin.

———. 2000. *Gathering Blue*. Boston: Houghton Mifflin.

MacLachlan, Patricia. 1993. *Baby*. New York: Delacorte Press.

Manes, Stephen. 1982. *Be a Perfect Person in Just Three Days*. New York: Clarion Books.

McGovern, Ann. 1999. *If You Lived 100 Years Ago*. New York: Scholastic.

Moody, Ralph. 1962. *Little Britches*. New York: Norton.

Naylor, Phyllis Reynolds. 1991. *Shiloh*. New York: Atheneum.

O'Dell, Scott. [1961] 1987. *Island of the Blue Dolphins*. New York: Scott Foresman.

Osborne, Mary Pope. 1996. *One World, Many Religions: The Ways We Worship*. New York: Knopf.

———. 1998. *The Hour of the Olympics.* New York: Random House.

———. 2001. *Christmas in Camelot.* New York: Random House.

Park, Barbara. 1997. *Skinnybones.* New York: Random House.

———. Junie B. Jones Series. New York: Random House.

Paulsen, Gary. 1994. *Mr. Tucket.* New York: Delacorte Press.

———. 1999. *Hatchet.* New York: Aladdin Paperbacks.

Pilkey, Dav. 1993. *Dogzilla: Starring Flash, Rabies, Dwayne, and Introducing Leia as the Monster.* San Diego: Harcourt Brace Jovanich.

———. 2001. *Captain Underpants and the Wrath of the Wicked Wedgie Woman: the Fifth Epic Novel.* New York: Blue Sky Press.

Porter, Connie. 1993. *Meet Addy: An American Girl.* Middleton, WI: Pleasant Company.

Pullman, Philip. 1999. *The Firework-Maker's Daughter.* New York: Arthur A. Levine Books.

Quindlen, Anna. 1998. *How Reading Changed My Life.* New York: Ballantine.

Raschka, Chris. 1993. *Yo? Yes!* New York: Orchard Books.

Rasinski, Tim. 2001. "Walking the Walk: Ourselves as Literate Persons." *Ohio Journal of English Language Arts* 41, no. 2 (spring): 84–85.

Ray, Katie Wood. 1999. *Wondrous Words: Writers and Writing in the Elementary Classroom.* Urbana, IL: National Council of Teachers of English.

Robinson, Barbara. 1965. *Trace Through the Forest.* New York: Lothrop, Lee & Shephard.

Routman, Regie. 2000. *Conversations: Strategies for Teaching, Learning, and Evaluating.* Portsmouth, NH: Heinemann.

Rowling, J. K. 1997. *Harry Potter and the Sorcerer's Stone.* New York: Scholastic.

Rylant, Cynthia. 1995. *The Van Gogh Café.* New York: Harcourt Brace.

Sachar, Louis. 1998. *Holes.* New York: Farrar, Straus and Giroux.

Scieszka, Jon. 1998. *Summer Reading Is Killing Me!* New York: Viking.

———. 1999. *It's All Greek to Me.* New York: Viking.

———. 2001. *Baloney (Henry P).* New York: Viking.

Segal, Erich W. 1970. *Love Story.* New York: Harper Row.

Simon, Seymour. 1993. *Autumn Across America.* New York: Hyperion Books for Children.

Speare, Elizabeth George. 1983. *The Sign of the Beaver.* Boston: Houghton Mifflin.

———. 2001. *The Witch of Blackbird Pond.* Boston: Houghton Mifflin.

Spinelli, Jerry. 1990. *Maniac McGee: A Novel.* Boston: Little, Brown.

———. 1997. *Wringer.* New York: HarperCollins.

Stevens, Janet. 2001. *And the Dish Ran Away with the Spoon.* San Diego: Harcourt.

Taberski, Sharon. 2000. *On Solid Ground: Strategies for Teaching Reading K–3.* Portsmouth, NH: Heinemann.

Tatum, Beverly Daniel, Ph. D. 1997. *"Why Are All the Black Kids Sitting Together in the Cafeteria?" And Other Conversations About Race*. New York: Basic Books.

Trelease, Jim. 2001. *The Read-Aloud Handbook*. 4th ed. New York: Penguin Books.

Walsh, Jill Paton. 1986. *The Green Book*. New York: Farrar, Straus and Giroux.

Weisner, David. 2001. *The Three Pigs*. New York: Clarion Books.

Wells, Rosemary. The McDuff Series. New York: Hyperion Books for Children.

Winthrop, Elizabeth. 1985. *The Castle in the Attic*. New York: Holiday House.

———. 1993. *The Battle for the Castle*. New York: Holiday House.

Wisniewski, David. 1998. *The Secret Knowledge of Grown-ups*. New York: Scholastic.

———. 2001. *The Secret Knowledge of Grown-ups: The Second File*. New York: HarperCollins.